Everything I Learned About Leadership I Learned From Filmmaking

Creativity and passion at work and in life.

by
William Azaroff

The events and conversations in this book have been set down to the best of the author's ability, although some names and details have been changed to protect the privacy of individuals.

Copyright © 2021 William Azaroff

All rights reserved. No part of this book may be reproduced in any form on by an electronic or mechanical means, including information storage and retrieval systems, without permission in writing from the publisher, except by a reviewer who may quote brief passages in a review.

ISBN: 9798470854926 (Kindle Edition)

Cover Design by Andrew Hess

First edition September 2021
Published by William Azaroff
www.azaroff.com

Table of Contents.

Prologue. 1
Do what you love… 6
Be an imposter. 12
You're not really in The Business. 20
Audition for the role. 27
Are you making it better, or just making it different? 33
Ask for feedback. 42
Understand the subtext. 47
Put a note on your fridge. 52
Eliciting great performances. 58
Choosing the music. 66
Get used to failing. 74
Killed with a fork. 81
Mission is everything. 85
The third take rule. 92
The 19th film festival. 98
Do your job. 104
Living in your car. 109
Faulkner, Einstein and Newton. 116
Learn to pitch. 124
Today's intern is tomorrow's executive. 129
Toss the script. 134
Understanding Shakespeare. 141
Kill your babies. 146
Tell your story. 151
Closing credits. 157
About the author. 160

Prologue.

I've had this idea bottled up within me for a long time: to correlate the abilities and aptitudes I have drawn on as an executive at a financial institution and as CEO of a successful not-for-profit with my early, formative years as an independent filmmaker. There are dots I connect between these two phases of my working life and there are lessons I draw upon on a daily basis even though I left filmmaking behind long ago.

I started writing and directing plays and then making videos and films in high school. As a teenager, I was surrounded by friends who were creative, ambitious and eccentric, and who inspired me to keep my creative desires front and centre. After a dozen years making films and producing plays, I made a move in the late '90s when web technologies were beginning to flourish. I spent the next dozen years working in digital production in Seattle, LA and then back in Vancouver, Canada where I grew up.

In ways I couldn't have predicted or even imagined, I ended up working for Vancity, a large community credit union with $30 billion in assets. Vancity focuses on delivering financial services in ways that contribute to community health, equity and empowerment. I rose through the ranks from doing web project management to overseeing all digital channels, made a lateral move to lead the Community Investment department and eventually to executive leadership positions. At one point, I led the largest division in the organization, made up of 1,800 people across 60 branches and central offices across Southwest British Columbia.

From there I was recruited to be CEO of Brightside Community Homes Foundation, a large not-for-profit with a quarter of a billion dollars in assets, providing affordable homes to over 1,000 people who struggle to meet the demands of market housing in Vancouver, one of the most unaffordable cities on the planet.

In so many ways, I could not be in a more different place than in my early twenties making independent films. Yet, on a daily basis, there are situations I encounter in which I draw on the lessons I learned as a struggling young filmmaker. There are parallels I see so clearly between these two branches of my career, even if they're not at first very obvious.

I don't know anyone else with the same career trajectory I have had. I get asked all the time how my career path has wound its way to where I am now and what lessons I would impart to others. In October 2012, I gave a talk at a conference in Nashville called *Everything I Learned About Leadership I Learned From Filmmaking*. It was such a cathartic experience to share my story and my lessons learned that I decided to turn it into a book to capture my experiences. I wrote this book because a creative background, although unusual, is in so many ways a fantastic foundation for broader positions in leadership.

Frankly, I wouldn't want to work for an organization that was run exclusively by former theatre geeks, but I often wish more buttoned-down companies had at least one executive like me: someone who brings a creative perspective, frames things differently and doesn't have the same tried and true MBA ways of seeking opportunities, addressing challenges and working through issues.

My uniqueness has served me well, and it leaves me pondering the *why*. Why, when we look for executives at our companies, do we look for people cut from the same cloth? What is it in my background that works so well at an executive leadership or board table? These are themes I have been exploring and wanting to share, because I think they illuminate a different way to gain skills and experience —far from the mainstream way most people learn at university and gain knowledge and perspective from their early career lessons.

—

There are too few people who bring (or feel they are allowed to bring) their passion and curiosity into the workplace. I worked in many places where I didn't feel like I belonged and in hindsight, I think it was because I felt like I couldn't be myself at work. Sometimes it felt like we were supposed to leave all that makes us unique and human at the door. Embracing that which makes us special, what brings out our passion, what draws upon our natural curiosity is a key under-appreciated trait in the workplace.

The reason for that, in part, is that we have too few leaders who allow for humanity in the office. Bringing a creative mindset has enabled me to embrace the benefits that different people carry with them and a desire to allow us all to be human and authentic at work. This is the style that I accidentally imported into the business workplace from the theatre and the filmset.

I have written this book to encourage others to follow their instincts and to draw on the parallels between what we love to do and what we do for work. The focused, pre-packaged and often frustratingly empty career advice that fills so many pages at airport bookstores yields lives that could be so much more joyous, surprising and enriching. I have found that the approach I have taken breeds resilience and adaptability to changing trends, markets and opportunities, which has served me very well.

It is worth noting that when I look back on my career journey now, with the benefit of hindsight, I see a lot of my confidence and comfort in taking risks was guided by an invisible hand I didn't understand at the time. I stumbled into opportunities and around barriers in ways I didn't appreciate when I was a young man. I would be remiss if I didn't recognize the role that privilege has played in my good fortune. I didn't understand it at the time and had no idea that the luck I experienced and chances I had, especially as someone climbing the corporate ladder without even a bachelor's degree, would be far less likely to occur if I were a woman, or Indigenous, or Black, or disabled, or part of the LGBTQ+ community. I don't want to take my privilege for granted or pretend it didn't play a starring role in my journey. I also believe that anyone who loves what they do and has passion and curiosity, is a far more attractive candidate and can create more opportunities for themselves than if they don't.

I hope this book will inspire you to do what you love, and to find parallels between parts of your life that today you may see as separate. The things that you do merely because they inspire and fulfill you can create lessons for your career as a leader that are rewarding and bring you joy.

Everything I learned about leadership, it turns out, I really did learn from making films. I think some of what I learned will be entertaining and of interest to others. I hope you enjoy!

—

Do what you love…

When I started to make films, it wasn't a conscious choice. I never decided to be a filmmaker. I followed my heart into it one step at a time from a childhood desire to be a theatre actor, to working on other people's films, to writing screenplays, to making films of my own. I didn't choose to be a filmmaker, it kind of chose me.

I loved narrative storytelling; I loved making art that people watched unfold over time. I loved working with a diverse array of people with disparate abilities, personalities and quirks to make something together and see a project reach fruition. I loved creating something collaboratively with a team of creative and resourceful people and showing it to an audience and sensing their reaction as they watched it in a dark theatre. I loved whatever prestige and attention came my way as a filmmaker, even if very few people actually ever saw my films.

Truth be told, I wasn't making very good films, but, *boy-howdy* did I love it. In all my time making films, I never equated my love for it with a pay-check. As long as I could scrape by and pay my rent and get some food, I was happy being able to focus on my films.

After a dozen or so years making films, I shifted into the emerging digital industry, a career choice made easier by my attitude. I found the work fun, and it piqued my curiosity while utilizing many of the core skills and relationships I had developed as a filmmaker.

—

As a young person, I was never very concerned with career choices. At five years old, I told my parents I wanted to act, which morphed into filmmaking sometime late in high school. I remember a well-intentioned—but rigidly-minded—high school guidance counsellor, Mr. Barabond, telling an entire ninth grade guidance class that we all needed to write three career choices on a piece of paper and pass them forward for his evaluation. I was stumped. I wrote "Actor" and then "Director" and then, still at a loss, wrote "Actor" once more. He told me those amounted to one choice in total and I needed two more. I went home and struggled to come up with anything else. I only ever came up with one other choice "Buisnessman", and even that I misspelled (which Mr. Barabond found entirely unimpressive).

I'm not sure I even knew what I meant at the time when I wrote the made-up job of "Buisnessman". It's funny to me thinking about this as CEO at Brightside, a very business-minded not-for-profit that by all measures I am now a genuine businessperson—perhaps exactly what I imagined when I struggled with my career choice list for Mr. Barabond.

Back in ninth grade, listening to The Smiths on endless repeat likely had some influence on the seriousness with which I observed Mr. Barabond. I doubt a single other person in that guidance class remembers that day at all. I'm sure that following my dreams and throwing career planning to the winds is exactly the *opposite* lesson Mr. Barabond meant to impart, but that's the main lesson I derived and reflect on to this day: Follow your passions and interests, take things one step at a time, try not to worry too much and it will all (hopefully) work out.

That guidance counsellor gave me a tremendous, albeit accidental, gift. Starting my career without worrying what exactly I was going to do—or how I was going to earn a living doing it—was a great start to my working life. At the same time, I learned that other people had strong opinions about what I *should* be doing with my life—that my career choice worried other people in ways that didn't cause me any concern.

—

When I was 22 years old and had just moved to Seattle and out on my own with my girlfriend (and now-wife) Amy for the first time, a friend of my father's, Irma, offered to take us out for lunch. Relatively early on during our walk to grab a bite, Irma started asking me increasingly pointed questions about my career choice of filmmaking. She grilled me on why didn't I get a degree in something useful like teaching and then pursue filmmaking in my spare time. It was a very tense afternoon, and because she was a friend of my father's I didn't do the one thing I wanted to, which was tell her to stuff it and leave. Instead, I went toe-to-toe with her for hours, defending my choices and my passion, and hoping to win her over. I did not accomplish my goal; she remained insistent that she knew what was better for me than I did. I had a sinking feeling that there would be a thorough report back to my father on what had transpired.

At the end of a long and stressful afternoon, we all went back to her place so Amy and I could fetch our things and I noticed a book on her bookshelf. It was titled, *Do What You Love, The Money Will Follow*. I threw up in my mouth.

I didn't know that little axiom at the time, but I did inherently believe that if I did what I loved, I'd do okay. I've always sensed that about my career, even though I now look back and see that it reeks of privilege. I didn't do what I did for the money, I just wanted to get by. The harder part, it turns out, is figuring out what you love to do in the first place.

Needing to demonstrate that I could make sound career choices to people like my high school guidance counsellor and my dad's friend, who failed to understand me, instilled in me the ability to ignore (or at least attempt to ignore — here I am over thirty years later still reflecting on all of this) feedback that wasn't right for me or my desires.

I'm sure it must have driven my parents nuts. I'm sure I would worry if my son went off into his career without a lot of planning or schooling. Yet, my experience demonstrates that simply following your heart and doing what you love is a phenomenal, if rare, thing.

—

In general, we worry a lot about our careers. We apply to the right schools, we stress over the important tests, we do community service to pad out our resumes. When I am asked how my career path led me to where I am today I see one recurring theme in the circuitous, unpredictable and absolutely non-replicable route my career has taken: Do what you love, check in periodically to make sure you still love it, examine and re-examine your priorities and stay focused on what you enjoy.

In all our striving to put together an impressive resume to get to the top of the heap, we overlook one major factor in finding success, a factor that I learned in spades making films and following my own star wherever it took me (beyond white, male privilege). I had passion and curiosity, and it has been those qualities that won me jobs I know I was far less qualified for than other people I was competing against. Passion and curiosity led to unpredictable opportunities and roles in which I had no direct experience, but I was unexpectedly well-suited for. It was my passion that was infectious, my creativity that people wanted on their teams and my curiosity that kept me humble and wanting to learn. These traits have always counted for more in my career than my education—which admittedly I don't have a lot of, having dropped out of university halfway through my undergrad to make films.

My energy, passion, curiosity, and creativity have counted for more than anything else. They have led me to be in the right place at the right time and to know interesting people. They have also created a kind of allergic reaction when I'm in the wrong job or at the wrong company. When my passion and curiosity have not been desired or appreciated at a job, I move on. I can't stay at a place that doesn't value that part of me that makes me *me*. My background has given me a strong sense of myself, and knowledge that I know *why* I am excited about the job I'm applying for or staying at the organization where I am working.

You can't necessarily teach these things, that is true, but you can lead with your heart as much as your head and develop a trust in your instincts that will strengthen that muscle and help it grow within you. You can build self-awareness to continuously challenge decisions when they don't work out, so that your instincts improve and you can learn to trust your intuition more and more.

—

Be an imposter.

At the start of my career, whenever I had a film idea that I couldn't resist moving forward with, I always had this twinge of, "*Who do I think I am?*" Whether I was writing, planning, in pre-production, bouncing ideas off people or asking for help, I often felt like a fraud. What made my idea so worthwhile that I thought actors, producers and technicians would come along for the ride with me to make my film?

Yet, each time I felt compelled to make a film, each time I had an idea that I honestly felt like I couldn't *not* make, I always found talented, capable people willing and sometimes even eager to sign up and join me. Sometimes that meant they worked on the project for free, as my budgets were extremely low and salaries were out of the question. People cashed in their vacation time, quit jobs they were ready to leave, took a break between gigs and borrowed time away from other pursuits to come along the journey with me.

It was always deeply humbling and gratifying, and something I never took for granted. I saw it as a barometer that I was doing something worthwhile, because I trusted that people weren't irrational and wouldn't do all this just for me. There was something about the story I wanted to tell, the project or the experience that pulled on them to invest their time. Through them, I clarified for myself that what we could create together was compelling, and I began to understand that it was my vision and passion for the project that sealed the deal.

Each time I started a film project, I felt this enormous sense of responsibility, because it wasn't just my life, my livelihood or my career that I was playing with. The stakes were an order of magnitude higher. I was responsible for other people now, so I had better believe that their time, effort and money were worth it.

That doesn't mean I didn't take leaps of faith. When I was twenty years old, a good friend of mine, Asaf, who was critical to my becoming a filmmaker, was making a film and asked me to be his editor. I had always been a good editor of my own projects, but up until that point we had shot and edited on video due to lack of funds. Asaf was the first of us to make the leap to 16mm film. I was in awe. When he asked me to edit his film, I could have told him honestly that even though I really wanted to, I had never cut on film before, and that I was sorry but I couldn't help him out. I didn't do that. Instead I eagerly accepted and was incredibly excited to work on my first real *film*.

I went to the library immediately (keep in mind, this was 1990, eight years before Google) and took out a bunch of books on 16mm film editing. I worked all this knowledge into my head over a couple of days. I told Asaf that I would need a day in the editing room by myself to get comfortable with the specific equipment. I walked into the editing room vibrating with excitement to get my hands on the 16mm Steenbeck editing machine. I spent that day with my borrowed library books taking what was in those pages and applying it to the equipment sitting in front of me. I made a ton of mistakes, but started to kind of get the hang of it. When Asaf showed up the next day ready to start, I am sure I was clumsy, but I faked it for a few days until I became (somewhat) proficient.

I'm sure Asaf knew I was faking it, but he was patient and kind. He knew that sometimes we have to fake it until we make it. That's still true of my professional stretch assignments.

As we move up the ladder, hopefully we know enough to do what is being asked of us, but that we may not have all of the skills we need to give us confidence. So we fake it and stumble our way through and learn quickly on the job.

That feeling of being an imposter, of being in over my head, still remains with me at times. Being in over your head is sometimes, and if you get it right, mostly a healthy thing. It is essential for testing limits to see if you have evolved to a point where you can take on new challenges and rise to new occasions. Every so often, we need to test that we have a solid enough footing on the high wire so that we can venture out another step.

The single biggest example of feeling like an imposter was when I was asked to take part in an executive leadership rotation at Vancity. This leadership rotation meant that three VPs at the credit union would each spend a year in the most significant executive position in the organization. I had been promoted to Vice President of Community Investment only a year-and-a-half earlier and had been working hard to operate at the level I felt like a VP should. I had focused on expanding my leadership, influence and ability to get things done in the organization. I was now asked to run all of our operating lines of business for one year. These were all of the people and in-person channels who helped the half a million members (customers) on a daily basis, including the branch network, call centre, wealth management, business banking and commercial real estate departments. I went from leading 30 people to leading 1,800 overnight.

Up to this point, I had been able to lead in a very personal way; I could bring my entire department together to meet and discuss topics that affected us. I moved from a position where I knew everyone, where we could discuss issues, and I could hear team-members' perspectives and opinions directly, to leading an incredibly large group of people in many different locations. I would never get to meet most of the people I was now leading, and their opinions would get filtered and edited through the hierarchy of the organization before reaching me. I was leading departments whose work I only understood at the surface level, whose daily activities I couldn't perform.

It was a huge leap, and oh wow, did I feel like an imposter. I came into the organization via my digital and marketing background. I hadn't worked in a branch, I hadn't done a business loan, I didn't have a certification in wealth management. I was totally faking it.

Because this was a one-year assignment, I had very little time to raise my game, develop leadership skills to manage through my direct reports and theirs and connect with as many people—directly or indirectly—as possible. My relationship with my employees-once-removed, those staff who reported directly to the people who reported to me, was essential. I made sure I met with each of them one-on-one at least once a quarter. This way they could hear directly from me and I could understand the needs of their business units. It enabled me to understand what was really going on, essential to staying connected and ensuring decision-making was relevant to the people closest to the members.

As you become more senior, you grow removed from the people who interact with your customers and work on the front line of what your organization does. The game of telephone that occurs at senior leadership can be folded in half if you engage with the right level of their management.

When I first became a VP and was learning the ropes at that level, I witnessed peers who were terrible micro-managers; they got lost in the weeds, got involved in issues that didn't require a VP. I also saw VPs who never understood what their people did, never dove deep enough to understand their team's work and stayed above the fray and were never very effective.

I learned that a key to successful leadership was knowing enough about what your team does every day, what they are experiencing and what gets in their way to effectively lead them. I feel very fortunate that I made so many lateral moves across different functional areas. Leaders I saw who were promoted within the team where they worked, overseeing functions that they knew intimately could easily fall victim to micro-managing. The thinking of, *I did this so well that I was promoted so I must know what's best for everybody* can lead to truly terrible leadership outcomes.

I struggled with the opposite problem. I made mistakes when I didn't understand the work well enough that I couldn't support my team with their challenges. Staff would come to me about a process that wasn't working or a challenge they had in their day-to-day duties and I couldn't help them directly.

Leadership, especially senior or executive leadership, requires you to know when to dive deep and hear directly from the people affected by the issues, so you can understand what's really going on. After gaining that understanding, and this is so critical, you have to know when to come back up to your senior level. I had to understand the experience of my people on the ground well enough to represent and lead them. I learned to dive deep where needed so I could help solve problems and come back up immediately.

That's the secret. As an executive, you need to stay at the right level as a leader and not risk disempowering your team, but know when to drop in, work through some details to provide clarity or ensure things that are broken get addressed and then, wait for it, come back up to your executive level, empowering others to execute the work.

—

That feeling of being a fraud disappeared over time and was overtaken by a feeling of immense gratitude for the opportunity to work with people who have very different skills to achieve great things together. Through digging in and learning the work of different departments, visiting business areas to meet as many of my new team as I could and understanding the complexities involved with running a highly regulated, community-oriented credit union, I gained knowledge, proficiency and—eventually—confidence.

In fact, when I haven't felt like an imposter for a long stretch, I realize that I am playing it too safe and need a change, to stretch myself and bring back my creativity. My experience with that feeling of safety came in my final months of leading the digital team at Vancity.

I had done digital work for a dozen years, and I was starting to become one of those leaders who was a *we tried that once and it didn't work* types. The kind of leader who inadvertently squashed creativity and innovation. It was time for me to get uncomfortable again, and so I took the leap from doing digital projects to working in the community investment area of the organization. I needed to get out of my comfort zone and feel like an imposter again.

We've all seen those employees who've been in their roles too long. In some that tenure can make them appear as detached. In others it manifests itself as arrogance. Or frustration or condescension. Or apathy. When I see people like that, I think that they've been in their positions too long. They need a change, a new challenge: perhaps a lateral move within their department, an assignment to a new department, or perhaps a change to a different company (as we'll cover in a later chapter, *Tossing The Script*).

My job as a leader is to have open discussions with my team-members, so we recognize those signs early and I can advocate for them to another manager. That needs to happen before they show signs of frustration, boredom or complacency—which can be incredibly damaging to an employee's reputation and hinder their growth. I was lucky that I changed roles and departments before that happened to me. I want to help others do the same, if they're willing to take a leap and try something new.

If you haven't felt like an imposter in a little while, perhaps it's time to leap out of your comfort zone. Time to find something you're passionate about, to jump into a 16mm editing bay even though you've never edited film before. Give yourself that feeling of being a creative beginner again. Try something that challenges you and your assumptions. Something that takes you from being the most experienced and knowledgeable person in the room to being the least experienced and most naive, curious and driven.

—

You're not really in The Business.

When I was starting to fall out of filmmaking, I had a singular moment that told me it was time to leave film behind. I had recently finished making a feature film and was looking for inspiration for my next project. It was during the dot.com era, and I was working as a digital producer at a small boutique web marketing agency focused on the entertainment industry. It was perhaps the single most creative place I have ever worked. It was small, maybe a dozen of us, but we worked on some incredible projects, and the couple who ran the place had a gift for getting the marketing departments at the movie studios to give us a lot of creative freedom.

One day, we were out at a local hot spot in West Hollywood having snacks and drinks, celebrating getting a proposal accepted by Disney. The waiter, obviously an actor trying to break into the business, was half-interestedly serving us (LA is full of people working in restaurants who need you to know this is only their day job until their career breaks through, which could happen at any moment).

He looked at us celebrating, and after taking our order, he asked us if we were in The Business. Suddenly, perhaps we might be interesting to him. If it were up to me, I would have told him that no, we were not in The Business. In my opinion, creating websites for movie studios to help sell more tickets was at least a few steps removed from The Business.

Instead, one of the two owners of the company told him that we were, in fact, in The Business. The waiter leaned in a bit, eyeing us closer. "What do you do?" he asked.

"We create websites for the movie studios. Right now we're celebrating that we landed *Finding Nemo*."

The waiter paused, thinking it over. What could we do for him? He eventually replied, "Oh, so you're not *really* in The Business." And he turned and left us.

I remember that moment well because there was so much wrong in that singular interaction. Both sides of the story wanted to be recognized as important—as belonging to The Business. Both were trying not just to impress the other, but to show that they were better than the other. I looked at my boss's deep need to impress a waiter at a random bistro in LA. I watched the waiter dismiss us, sorry he invested time in us because we couldn't help his career—disappointed that he got his hopes up for a second. To him, we were nobodies.

In that moment, I think the very last part of me that still thought of myself as a filmmaker was turned off of The Business. I started seeing a therapist at that point, because I felt so defined, internally and externally, by filmmaking, that I had to re-familiarize myself with what I was about. For me, if I had pushed through—in spite of my own growing awareness that although I enjoyed filmmaking, I was never going to be great at it—I would slip from persistence into delusion (more on that later).

—

As a filmmaker, I never really decided when to make a new film. There was never a moment when the thought occurred to me to start a new project. I would find myself writing a script in my spare time, talking about it with friends, scribbling some notes and just thinking about it all the time. It would work its own way through my consciousness. I didn't sit down and decide it was time to write something. I wrote when I couldn't *not* write.

I also had a seamless transition from writing to producing. I made a film when I was so devoted to an idea or a story that I realized I was waist deep in pre-production and just *was* making a film. When I was excited about what I was writing, I would find myself talking to actors about roles, looking at possible locations where I could shoot and speaking to people about the production. I made films because it was as natural to me as getting dressed, eating and going about my day. It was simply what I did.

At some point that sense of destiny dissipated. I started thinking about the next film I *should* make. That natural impulse had vanished. I had always made films when I couldn't *not* make them, and now I was searching around to find a story to tell. It occurred to me that I only really needed to make another film because I had defined myself so successfully as a filmmaker in other people's eyes. I didn't want to let them down. But filmmaking had always been something I did just for me. I began to realize that I had lost my way. I started to feel desperate, and desperation wasn't going to lead me to anywhere I wanted to be.

I didn't feel like the world needed another filmmaker; I made the films I felt compelled to make. For many years I had a goal of making a feature film, something of substance and duration. After years of making shorts, I wanted to push myself to tell a singular story over ninety minutes. After finally completing my feature film, *The Engagement Party*, that feeling dissipated. It evaporated. I worked on some other scripts, dabbled in some projects, but that feeling never returned. I had achieved my goal of making a feature, and I felt accomplished and complete.

I spent my 20s earning very little money, dedicating myself to where I felt a great calling. At 30, I started understanding that what I was great at was producing—bringing people together and making things happen. I could inspire people to action. Being truthful with myself, I saw that I wasn't a great screenwriter or director, but I was a great producer.

I was very lucky. I often reflect that there is an alternative reality where I kept pushing in the world of film, trying to prove myself to others instead of being honest with myself. In this alternate world I have utterly failed and have nothing to show for it.

I was lucky that I got swept up in the transition in society towards digital tools and technologies. Being an admirer of the film producers and the studio founders at the turn of the previous century, I recognized a pattern. Just as those studio pioneers in the early 1900s saw film as an important new medium that others had yet to recognize—that these new motion picture tools were part of a larger societal transformation—I recognized the once-in-a-lifetime moment that this digital revolution represented and decided to jump in.

I'm glad I did, because the people who hired me, who gave me support and took chances on me, saw that my skills from a decade of experience in filmmaking were transferable. Suddenly, instead of spending my time swimming against the flow and pushing and pushing to make my projects happen, I was going with the current. For the first time, I was getting paid good money to lead projects that I found rewarding, challenging and interesting. I swung on a fragile vine out of indie filmmaking and into digital production.

Shaking things up once in a while is a very important thing. As we discussed, it can open up new opportunities that you hadn't previously considered. Or at the very least it can reinforce that you're doing the right thing. I have experienced both.

—

When I was 40, I went through a low point when my sense of commitment to my work at Vancity was pretty shallow. The usual engagement I had felt at work was vanishing and I was starting to feel a deep itch to do something else. I just didn't know what I should do. I needed to figure that out. Again, desperation loomed.

I took a day off work and scheduled a whole bunch of informational interviews with people to get their advice and perspective and to see if I could line up some consulting work. I had a series of phone interviews throughout the morning with people on the East Coast that were very promising. It seemed like I could line up some consulting gigs quickly and pretty easily. That was exciting. In the afternoon I had some meetings downtown in person. My last meeting was with an executive at a consulting company whom I trust and admire. He painted a very exciting picture of a consulting opportunity combining finance and digital communications. I was feeling sold on the opportunity that consulting presented. As we wrapped up our chat he made an offhand comment that hit me hard. He said that I could probably be very successful and *only* have to travel two weeks out of each month.

Of course, with the consulting lifestyle comes a lot of travel. Travel to pitch clients, travel to do work or present results. I love my home life and work-life balance is very important to me. I work with passion and so burnout is a real risk for me if I don't pace myself. In that moment, I wondered if I was cut out for the consulting life. I came home after that meeting and made a list of what I need from a job and what I would hate. After making the two lists and comparing them, I realized that my job at the time at Vancity fit my "*what I need from a job*" list extremely well. The feeling of desperation dissipated.

I found a renewed sense of commitment to my work after going through that process of self-evaluation, and my desire to leave to explore other things went away. Soon after that, perhaps as a coincidence and perhaps due to my renewed commitment and enthusiasm, I was offered a very exciting new opportunity to move to the Community Investment team and I ended up staying at the organization for several more years.

I know lots of people who stayed in a position or at a company for too long and became disengaged and even angry. That anger may well be the result of desperation — of feeling like you have few options, or that you have invested too much time to leave. Some people can stay put and continue to find their work challenging and interesting and don't start feeling a creeping resentfulness or desperation. Others need a change every so often to shake things up (like we discussed in the chapter *Be An Imposter*).

We don't do ourselves or the people we work with any favours by staying put longer than we should. Many of us have busy lives, busy careers, busy families. It is easy to feel stuck and desperate. Sometimes, for your own sake, you just need to go easy on yourself, examine and re-examine your priorities, ensure you're not trying to prove anything to anyone or be anything you're not, and figure out your next move. You should be doing what you do for all the right reasons. Otherwise you risk being like that waiter and my former boss, arguing over who really belongs and trying to avoid their own feelings of desperation.

—

Audition for the role.

There was a time in my youth when all I wanted in life was to be an actor. Growing up, that was my dream. I was lucky, because when I was in high school, Vancouver was emerging as a major location for film and TV production. I had several friends who landed decent roles in TV shows and movies.

When I was 17, the pilot for a new show called *21 Jump Street* filmed in my high school. Pretty much everyone at the school who wanted to be an extra could become an extra. I jumped in, got hired and was hooked. I loved the experience of being on a film set, watching the actors and the crew and feeling the positive, fun and frenetic energy. I was even promoted to be a stand-in for Peter DeLuise, one of the main actors on the show. This seemed like an amazing opportunity at the time and paid an impressive four times the rate an extra earned.

After that experience my desire to act only increased. I managed to get an agent, had headshots made, and started auditioning for roles. I was sure I would land every part I went out for. I was exceedingly confident.

But I didn't land anything. Everyone I auditioned for passed on me and cast someone else. I took it very personally and found the rejection hard to stomach, especially as a teenager. After a few auditions, I gave up. That was the start of my desire to write, direct and produce instead of act. I found it too hard to be at the mercy of others, and to feel stinging rejection. I wanted to be in the driver's seat instead.

As I got into filmmaking and started working with talented professional actors, I learned a very valuable lesson from them. When you audition for a role, the director and casting director already have that character cast in their minds. The director has been living with the character for a while, imagining them vividly within the script pages. They know the type of actor they are looking for. Not necessarily every nuance, but they have a feel for who the character is and need to find the actor who most closely matches what they picture.

When an actor gets in front of them to read, it's an inherently vulnerable experience. They stand on their own, reading lines with someone they've never met, are given maybe 15 minutes and then are asked to leave. It feels shitty. And the frequent "no"s they hear can be profoundly demotivating.

In reality, those "No"s aren't meant as a rejection of the actor or statements on their talent. It's merely about finding the right match. The director is seeking someone who fits what's in their imagination. They will look at scores or hundreds or perhaps even thousands of people until the character they envision is standing right there in front of them. It isn't that all of the other actors are bad or untalented. It's that they weren't as close of a match.

When I began to understand that, my entire sense of the auditioning process changed. Not getting cast in a role wasn't a rejection or a statement of someone's talent, or lack of talent. It was about finding the actor who was closest to the character. Seasoned actors taught me that their job is to present themselves and their talents in the best possible light to see if they are similar enough to the invisible character in the director's imagination. They might be the one, but odds are likely that they won't be.

A good actor comes to the audition from a position of strength and confidence, presenting themselves for a potential match. That's a lesson I brought with me into the interview process.

—

When I lead an interview process, I want the people on the interview panel with me to create a sense of calm and safety so the person being interviewed can show up at their best. I want to see that person at their most confident, articulate and professional so I can assess them in their best light. Even seasoned leaders can get flummoxed and nervous at interviews. All we want is to show up at peak performance and to display our most authentic and unique selves so we stand the greatest chance of landing the job.

When I'm conducting an interview, my favourite opening question is, "*Why you, why this role, why now?*" I want to tease out why this person is applying for this specific role at this time in their career. I want to see if they've thought about what they bring and why this job is something they want to do.

If that answer falls flat it's usually because the job seeker isn't clear on why they want this specific job, want to work at that organization or why this is the right point in their career to make this particular leap. They may be shooting out lots of resumes to see what sticks. I want someone who's done their research on the organization and the role and has thoughts about why they want to make this move at this time.

When I interview for jobs, I want to present myself in the best way possible. Interviewers are seeking someone who will bring the skills they need, but equally important is that they are seeking someone who will be a suitable fit for the organization's culture. As someone with an unconventional resumé, I want to make sure I'm super-clear on why I want the job and what I bring. I also want to make sure that my non-MBA experience is viewed in a positive light—that will tell me a lot about whether the organization's culture is one I am interested in.

When you interview, your task is to present yourself to different organizations and to different hiring managers until you fit what that person is looking for.

When people I know are prepping for a job interview and they want my advice, they ask me what I think the interviewers might be looking for. I flip this around and ask them to articulate what they bring to the role and to the organization.

—

Whenever you hire someone, you're adding a missing ingredient to the make-up of the team as a whole. I look at the skills, attributes, behaviours and experience of the existing team and think about what would complement and expand their capacity and excellence. For the last several years, I have been hiring managers, directors and VPs. This can become a bit of a game of three-dimensional chess. Things I think about when hiring include: What does the team need in their leader? What kind of person would stretch their peers, my other direct reports? What kind of diversity would this new person bring to the team? How does this hire fit into the cross-section of all the management at this level in the organization? Might I be hiring a future senior executive or even CEO?

When I say fit, I don't mean I hire people just to fit in with the existing culture or talent. Sometimes a new person can expand the knowledge and experience of the existing team and by fitting in, this means they may be very different from who else is already in place.

I advise others to think through the kinds of questions they may encounter in an interview and have good, authentic answers beforehand. That's why I believe cover letters are so much more valuable than resumes. I want to hear the narrative of why the person is applying, not just a list of work and educational experiences. The cover letter is a much better way to get a sense of the person. A good cover letter will already give me a good sense of "*Why them, why this role, why now?*" A good cover letter and resume combo, when they fit what I am looking for, will make me excited to meet the person behind them.

Whether you are auditioning or interviewing, the main thing you can do is be clear on why you are applying, what you bring to the role, how this position fits into your own career trajectory and convey that clarity as effectively as you can. If you don't get the job, however, it isn't a personal rejection or necessarily a statement on your talent or hire-ability.

—

Are you making it better, or just making it different?

When you're a filmmaker, you often get asked to read other people's scripts. Lots and lots of scripts. Every script you read will make you a better writer. Each script is full of lessons about what to do, a glimpse into how others do what they do, or—at the very least—what not to do, what mistakes to avoid. Every script you read will either make you realize how much harder you have to work to be the writer you can be, or it will help you realize how far you've come to be the writer you are.

For me, it meant people approached me from all corners, somehow overlooking the fact that I could barely get my own films made, hoping that somehow I could help them make theirs. Over time, I became pretty good at reading scripts and giving feedback.

After reading many, many scripts and conveying my thoughts to different aspiring writers, I learned that giving good feedback is a skill. As I developed into a people-leader, giving feedback seemed to me to fall into three types:

The first is *Instruction*. This is needed when a writer is just beginning and is learning how to write a screenplay and develop into a decent writer. This is also true of employees new to a job, organization or role. They need to learn how to do their job.

The second is *Performance Management*. This is needed when a writer needs help to fix a broken or problematic script. This is also true for employees who are having issues at work and need to get things into shape or their job may be on the line.

The third is *Coaching*. That is what I am focusing on here, helping people make their scripts better. This assumes they know how to write; they don't have a script that is off the rails, but simply need feedback to make their script clearer and truer to what they are trying to communicate.

As a leader, I do all three, but I love to be able to coach a staff-member to help them up their game.

—

Before giving feedback, before cracking open the script or even agreeing to read someone's work, it is best to assess what kind of feedback that writer is looking for. It means listening closely to whether you are being asked to simply read a script as a courtesy read, or whether you are being asked for feedback. There's a big difference.

There were times when a screenwriter wanted me to read their script but didn't want feedback. Perhaps they wanted to show off their talents, or lacked the confidence it takes to ask for and receive feedback. Perhaps they were scared and just didn't know how to ask. I learned to avoid those situations and politely decline the courtesy read. Life is too short to read a script and not give input. If they, for example, wanted me to produce their film but not collaborate or give input into the script, then I knew I wasn't the right person for them.

Instead, I looked for people who asked for feedback. If I was going to spend a couple of hours reading their work, deliberating on it and thinking about what would make that story better, then I wanted to have an impact on the writer's ability to move closer to a sale, an option (an option is when a studio or producer pays a writer a small sum for the exclusive rights to the script for a limited period, taking it off the market while they deliberate or negotiate), the start of production or whatever it was the writer wanted.

For what it's worth, I also knew writers who wouldn't show their work to anyone for fear of being plagiarized. But that's silly. You can't sell or make a film without showing others your work—investors, producers, agents, executives, actors. Find people you trust and then take the risk of being brave. Otherwise, you'll never get better or move forward.

Nothing can put a writer in a more vulnerable position than showing something they've written to another person and asking for feedback. That display of vulnerability has to be respected, even if the actual writing itself may not be very good. If you're feeling petty, perhaps what you'd really like to tell the writer is that they lack talent and that they should give up their pursuit of writing. But rarely does that approach lead to results any reasonable person would hope for.

Most times when I received feedback, people were not actually giving me input to make my script better, they were just making it different, turning it into the script *they* would have written. By the time I asked someone I respected for feedback, I had been working hard on a script usually for weeks and months, making choices, spending time to make it as good as I could, but had hit some kind of limit and knew it could be better.

Bad advice ultimately led me away from the themes and ideas I wanted to explore in my film and the screenplay became muddier, murkier. It became about the reader's vision, not about mine, It was about them, and not about me. When someone seeks coaching, they need that experience to be focused on them and not on the coach. Great coaching elevates.

There is an enormous difference between good, meaningful, actionable feedback and input that is not useful, misses the mark or comes from a less well-intentioned place. Whenever I gave feedback to others that was focused more on what I wanted to tell the writer, rather than understanding what feedback they specifically wanted or needed to hear, I regretted it.

That's not to say that I didn't say things the writer didn't want to hear; it means I was sensitive to what they were asking of me and tried my best to ascertain what they needed. There's no point telling someone something they're not willing to hear. You have to find a way to help them process challenging feedback.

My experience giving feedback on writers' screenplays has directly benefited me as a people leader. A big part of my job today is to give feedback on performance, attitudes and behaviours in the workplace.

Giving feedback to a writer and to a direct report is very similar. Sometimes you'd like to just lay it on an employee when they're not doing what you'd like. You'd like to just be totally honest and tell them the unvarnished truth, but that isn't going to have the effect you desire. You play a significant role in the development of their entire career, both working with you and well beyond. What you say and how you say it (as well as *when* you say it, but we'll deal with that later) may inhibit that employee from trusting you and asking you for feedback ever again. It may keep them from asking any manager for feedback for years to come, especially if they're just beginning their career.

You may be afraid to comment on topics that are emotional or highly subjective. Holding back, however, won't help that writer develop their script into something better, or that direct report into a stronger employee.

Just because an employee comes to you with an issue doesn't mean they want your feedback. Similar to how I found that some writers would ask me to read their script but didn't ask for my input, some employees don't ask for feedback. Maybe they're afraid or insecure or don't know they should ask. Maybe they're trying to work it out for themselves and just want a coach to help them process possibilities and decisions. I have learned that when I give feedback to a writer who doesn't ask for it, my unsolicited feedback is bad news. Sometimes very bad news. Sometimes it can end friendships and business relationships.

—

There is a zen philosophy I adhere to and find meaningful: A teacher can only teach when the student invites them to teach. I don't assume people want to learn from me unless I am invited to share my opinion and perspective.

So, I listen to my staff carefully. Are they venting? Are they telling me something just to get it out there? Or are they asking for feedback? If they aren't asking for feedback, I jockey the conversation, to see if a little nudge can open up that invitation; if it doesn't come, I leave it there. Perhaps we're at a stage in our professional relationship when we're sizing each other up and still building trust. To give feedback at that juncture might prevent them from seeking feedback in the future. In those cases, I will gently let staff know that I have some feedback for them if they want to hear it, to get that line of thinking started.

I should note that this is different from dealing with performance issues. That's my job—to let staff know if there are significant gaps or behavioural issues that are impacting their performance or affecting the rest of the team. I'm talking more about the coaching that can help open up greater potential.

When the invitation for feedback does come—and this is critical—I think hard about the feedback they specifically need. I think about the writer who shows me their script. I don't give them feedback on the script they could have written, or the script I would have written, or the script they almost wrote. I really get into their script—the story they are trying to tell—and give feedback to make *that* script better.

Some of the worst moments I've had with my bosses over the years is when they gave me advice counter to where I wanted my career to go. I've had bosses who wanted me to develop parts of myself that I didn't deem very important. The moments of coaching that work best for me are when a boss takes the time to understand me and helps me lean into my strengths so that I become a more polished and excellent version of myself, rather than try to push me into areas where I may never really excel. That advice creates exhaustion and drives me off course, similar to bad script advice, rather than leaning in to help a script go further into the territory it is trying to explore.

I believe strongly that it is critical to understand what journey a person is on, so my coaching can help them on their own journey, and not tell them what I would do if I was in their shoes. Otherwise, I'm being selfish and unfair. Feedback is not about me, and I won't make it about me.

Employees are on a path, and I'm along for a part of their path. Do they know their path? Have they shared it? Have I asked? How do I connect with them, so I can help them along the journey they're on? How do I best attempt to align that journey with the organization's journey? How do I avoid telling them what I would do, and instead reflect on what they should do given their circumstances?

As a creative leader who maintains empathy whenever possible, I find giving feedback exhausting, because I'm listening so carefully. I choose my timing and feedback for greatest efficacy. When it works, I can tell it is very effective. Just like when I would help someone break through a script challenge; it unleashed incredible energy, potential, clarity and productivity.

This style of leadership requires a lot of patience, curiosity, silence, deep listening and a remarkable amount of empathy. It requires us to be interested in the big picture of what the organization is trying to achieve and an understanding of what any given employee wants and trying to find alignment between the two. If alignment can't be found, it is critical to name that. We are all better off if a disengaged employee finds their own way into a different job or another company where they are happier and more fulfilled.

I take the responsibility of managing people very seriously. It's an honour and privilege to play a key role in that person's professional (and, to some degree, personal) life. If I do my job right, it may impact them in all kinds of amazing ways for years to come.

I think about the best bosses I've ever had, and, like the great teachers I've had, they have had an impact on me far greater than the amount of time we spent in each other's company. They challenged me and supported me; they helped me grow, to achieve new things, to figure out what I wanted—even if the process of figuring that out led me away from reporting to them, perhaps out of that company entirely and on to other opportunities.

Looking at it from the opposite perspective, one way of impacting an employee, and in some cases the entire organization, is losing key talent because of poor management. I have observed this many times and I think we've all experienced it as employees. The negative side of this situation is, well, we all know the expression: *You don't quit your job, you quit your boss.*

If I do my job right, hire the right people, listen to them carefully to understand their ambitions and perspective and think hard about how I can help make their script better, then we establish a lot of trust—a strong bond to work together as a high-functioning team. We work together, learn a lot from each other, and can make all of our scripts better.

—

Ask for feedback.

In order to be a filmmaker, you also have to be willing to be vulnerable and show people your work and ask for feedback. It can be hard to do, to take something you've been working on, perhaps in isolation, and bring it to someone else to adjudicate. It requires a level of bravery that is sometimes difficult to summon. But it absolutely must be done. When I was making a film, I used to intentionally seek out people whose opinions I craved, but whose styles or judgement were different from mine.

In the last chapter we talked about giving feedback. Now we'll focus on asking for feedback. Seeking feedback is a critical part of our development as people, co-workers and especially as leaders. Asking for feedback can be difficult and even fraught with challenging emotions. I have also seen times when asking for feedback comes across as disingenuous and inauthentic.

I sometimes made the mistake of asking for feedback from people I felt I should, but whose opinions I didn't really respect. Perhaps they had shown me their scripts in the past, or we were friends or they repeatedly pestered me to let them see my script and wore me down and so I felt a sense of obligation, of duty to show it to them. That never went well, because I didn't actually want their feedback, and wasn't committed to the process of obtaining that feedback. I was just going through the motions.

I have also made the mistake of seeking feedback from people who looked up to me. I chose them because I knew their feedback would stroke my ego and make me feel good about what I had spent many months pouring myself into. Sometimes I chose people whose opinions were too much like my own, and the end result suffered because the writing didn't get worked through enough. I didn't obtain the critical feedback I needed to take the script to the next level. The feedback didn't demand excellence. It may have been immediately gratifying to hear nice things about my writing, but ultimately, it was lazy on my part. Great scripts, like diamonds, require pressure to squeeze them into shape and crystallize them into something beautiful.

Part of the way leaders grow, uncover blind spots and develop is to consistently request feedback. We need to get comfortable seeking and receiving feedback and gain the self-reflection and self-awareness required to improve how we lead and conduct ourselves. That's part of creative leadership, to desire input from people whose feedback we crave, but who we may not always agree with, or who share our perspectives.

One of the great leaders I worked for taught me an important lesson through her actions. Every few months, she asked me how she was doing as my manager and as a leader. She used to tell me, "Feedback is a gift. I always want feedback as long as you don't make me cry." I remember the exact moment when she first asked for my feedback because it took me by surprise — I had never had a manager ask me that in my career. And yet, it is such a profoundly simple question: *How am I doing?* How had I never been asked that before?

I learned from her leadership style that asking for feedback creates trust and reduces those moments when your behaviours aren't received in the ways you had hoped. Asking that question will reduce the management equivalent of having spinach in your teeth or walking around with your zipper undone.

When I have a healthy rapport with a co-worker or direct report, I'll ask whether I handled a meeting well, or how I showed up in a difficult conversation. I ask for feedback on strategies and briefing notes for the board. Like all feedback, it is best when I ask for input that is specific and timely, and so I try and ask focused questions to ensure I am doing well and don't overlook blind spots in my leadership.

I have started peer mentoring groups and invited people into them with whom I feel safe enough to have open, vulnerable dialogue, but who will challenge me to dig deeper and discover what's getting in my way. By engaging people who think differently from me, I have developed filters to receive the good feedback and leave behind the less relevant.

Developing these filters is critical because not all feedback is worthwhile. We have to examine it all and not reject good feedback just because it's hard for us to hear. Likewise, we shouldn't focus on feedback that isn't right for us. We need the self-awareness and resilience to know the difference. I have learned to ignore the type of feedback that we discussed in the chapter *Are You Making It Better, Or Just Making It Different?*—feedback from people who are trying to change my script to theirs. I leave behind input that is well-intentioned, but less relevant to me, and glean everything useful I can from their feedback.

But it's not enough to simply ask for feedback. It is the process of turning the feedback over and over in your mind, that act of self-reflection and trying to extract maximum value from any critique you receive that is essential to developing as a stronger leader.

When I showed people my script or an early cut of a film, I chose the people carefully. As my experience and maturity made me more confident, I chose people who I knew would tell me what I needed to hear. In my earlier days when I was less sure of myself, I chose people who would blow smoke and reaffirm what I wanted to hear.

When I requested feedback, I started asking myself: Would they say it like it is, or would they hold back? Can they deliver their feedback honestly, but with kindness? Do they know how to look at a rough cut and see beyond the blemishes to what I'm trying to achieve, or will they get caught up in the imperfections still to be ground out through the editing and post-production process? Do they bring a different set of perspectives that I haven't heard before?

As I write this book, I want the tough feedback from my early readers and editors that may require me to spend another month or two on rewrites when I thought (and hoped) I was done, if it makes the whole book better. As leaders, we should not just be willing, but craving to hear feedback from the teams we lead and from peers we work with, so that we can overcome our internal obstacles and take our abilities to new levels.

—

Understand the subtext.

When an actor or director reads through a script, they read it differently from how most people read something. They are constantly looking at the subtext—looking behind the words on the page for the themes and meanings the writer is trying to convey. This is one of the most important things they can do with a new script, to understand the elemental truths the writer is evoking.

The more nuanced and interesting the subtext, the more engrossing and meaningful the script. Subtext isn't just for arthouse and independent films. Even an action film, a horror movie, any popcorn flick, has subtext and can illuminate deeper meanings. Films with clear subtext, thoughts and through-lines that boil just below the surface, only seen obliquely, tend to be the movies that define their genre.

The reason for this is very simple. A script, a play, a novel, and for that matter a painting, a sculpture, a dance, a symphony—any work of art—strives to communicate meaning. The reason we as a species are drawn to stories and to art is to understand our condition in this world. We want to better understand who we should trust and who we shouldn't, what life means and how we can understand and contextualize all the love and joy and pain and suffering we experience.

Stories are our way of unpacking what happens to us and why. Enduring works of creative expression have a hidden meaning the audience or observer gets to discover for themselves. Those moments of discovery are what make art so satisfying to the audience; they get to experience the piecing together of a puzzle of meaning.

We go to the theatre to see a story and characters, but what sticks with us and keeps us turning the story over in our minds after the lights come up is the subtext. That's the sticky part.

Having said that, if a film was all subtext and that subtext was spoken and pointed to directly rather than, as the name indicates, existing below the surface, hidden in what isn't said directly, it would be ten minutes long. It would also be boring as hell, and no one would pay to see it. The lights would dim in the theatre, an actor would come on screen and say the thing the film is really about, explain what the meaning is (*"love is painful, but necessary"*) and then the credits would roll. It would be a lecture or a tutorial and not a story. It is subtext that keeps an audience guessing, what keeps them hooked.

As a director, you get used to scribbling about the subtext in the margins of the screenplay. Why is this character saying this line? Why is she so intent on obtaining the thing she's searching for? Why does he act that way to the other character? What does this scene really mean?

What may seem like small talk in a scene between two lovers is really something quite profound about their feelings for each other and the way they see the world.

—

As humans, we seek meaning. In a corporate context, the companies we work for have visions, missions and strategies they are pursuing. As leaders—especially as creative leaders—our job is to make sure we understand those words, and what their subtext is. It is in many ways no different than the job of a director. The better we understand the subtext in these vision and mission statements and strategies, the meanings below the surface that connect the dots and show the way forward, the more effectively we can be good employees, co-workers and leaders.

Some organizations lend themselves to more meaningful subtext than others. A shallow script won't yield much subtext for the actor to explore. It simply is what it is. A company whose only motive is maximizing shareholder value won't allow employees to create a story of meaning for themselves as to why they do what they do, and why they stay. A script with great subtlety and meaning will enable the actors, director, cinematographer, editor and others to bring out hidden meanings lying below the surface to help the film resonate with audiences and rise above. Those are the films that stay with us long after we have left the theatre. I believe people want to work for organizations with meaning, where the purpose affects society and the community. Those organizations with a mission will inspire greater commitment and productivity.

I once worked for a web marketing company that was a kind of digital sweatshop. In order to meet the deadlines the account executives set with the clients, staff had to work 60, 70 or more hours a week to stay on schedule. I remember working a 30-hour *weekend* to ensure a movie studio had a website to review on Monday morning for the rightfully forgotten Kevin Costner vehicle *Dragonfly*. Why? All because an executive at the firm had decided on a deadline without consulting the team for feasibility. I went to work one day at 8am and came home the next day at 3pm. I only left the office when I reached across to point out something on a colleague's screen and caught a whiff of myself and thought, *Oh man, go home!*

That 30-hour weekend was a key lesson for me on why I wanted to be working for mission-centred organizations. The reason why a group of skilled and talented designers, developers and producers spent their weekend working was because an account exec promised a deadline to please his bosses so the owners of the company could squeeze out greater profits. No senior leader of the company explained why this situation unfolded the way it did, it was just an unspoken expectation that staff would do whatever was necessary to meet deadlines created without their input. That weekend marked a tipping point in my own relationship with working for profit-driven companies.

I quit that marketing firm shortly afterwards, having felt exploited. On my last day, in one of the most amazing displays of solidarity I had ever experienced, one of the designers had created an image of me in the style of old Russian propaganda posters and titled it Che-zaroff. Every employee across the company put it up as their computer wallpaper for the day. I was very moved and felt that my defiance had, in fact, been an important act of leadership, emerging from my passion and curiosity. Although I didn't manage any staff, I felt like I was seen as a leader.

A strong mission empowers leaders to create a strong and compelling subtext for their staff.

When a new leader joins our organization, we should invest time with them to help them understand the mission and strategy right from the get-go, to make sure they are aligned with that mission. A leader's job is to ensure their staff are on the same page so they all make decisions in line with the business or organization's purpose and effectively move strategies forward. When they don't—and we've probably all experienced this—it feels like being on a boat where different people are rowing in different directions. There is a feeling resembling movement, but nobody's going anywhere very quickly. When meaning isn't clear, productivity suffers.

Just like a director discussing the subtext of a scene with her actors to ensure the interplay between their characters is coherent, understandable and exciting, we need to walk our staff through our organization's core strategies. We may each bring our own spin to the subtext, but just like two actors can't be in a successful scene together if they have radically different views of what the script is about, the organizational leader must also bring consistency to staff's understanding of the mission, vision and values. Both the director and the company leader need to put in the hard work to ensure that everyone is on the same page and sees the script's meaning in the same way.

—

Put a note on your fridge.

In the world of creative pursuits, there are two types of people: those who do, and those who talk about doing. I remember one of my pet peeves when I was making films was going to local film events and meeting someone who, when they learned I was in the middle of making a film, replied with, "Oh yeah, I have a film I want to make too." Often this comment would strike me hard when I was in the middle of the long slog of filmmaking, getting a million little details ready and working day and night to make things happen.

This comment would rub me the wrong way because here I was doing it, putting everything I had into my project, and they were equating the doing with the talking about doing. This was in the late '90s; it was a time when the historic high costs of filmmaking were dropping exponentially with the introduction of digital film technology. The barriers to getting a film made were collapsing and I would think, "Don't talk about the film you want to make, go make it."

I reflect on this as I finish this book. I had been wanting to write a book for many, many years. When I met someone who had written a book, I didn't respond with, "Yeah, I have a book I want to write too." I responded with, "That's awesome, good for you!" They were doing something I was just dreaming of, and I needed to appreciate the difference between dreaming and doing.

When making films, one little trick I used to get myself from the talking to the doing, was to put a note on my fridge with a date on it. That date may be when I wanted to finish a first draft, or when I would start shooting, or when the final edit would be done. I wanted to hold myself publicly accountable.

Admittedly, a note on my fridge isn't the most public display of accountability, so I would also tell people that date. Lots of people. There's nothing worse than running into someone you haven't seen in three months and have them say, "Hey, did you finish that screenplay by the end of June like you said you would?" and having to look them in the eye and start making excuses. I want the public shaming if I set a realistic but challenging goal and miss it.

I did the same thing with this book. In fact, I did more than post a note on my fridge or tell a few people the date when I aimed to complete a draft. With social media, I could tell more people than I ever used to when I made films. I wrote a blog post declaring that I was writing this book and when I aimed to have a first draft done. I cross-posted that to LinkedIn, Twitter and Facebook. I wanted others to hold me accountable. I wanted external pressure, to hold myself accountable.

It worked great, just as I'd hoped; I would bump into people and they would ask how the book was coming along and if I was going to meet my deadline. I had an intern on my team while I was working on my first draft, and he asked me if I was going to meet my intended date. I was surprised he knew about my book, so I must have looked a little shocked. He immediately started backtracking, scrambling in case he had insulted me, adding that in my blog post I had specifically requested that people hold me accountable. He thought he had overstepped, but I thought that was awesome—here was this intern afraid he had pissed off the VP, and, actually, I was delighted and told him so. I was being held accountable, just as I requested.

—

I used to know two writers: Peter and Terry. Peter was much more talented than Terry. I would read Peter's short stories and they were fantastic, especially considering he was probably 19 or 20 at the time. Terry's work, on the other hand, was obvious and derivative—it was stereotypical.

Despite his talents, Peter didn't produce much. He would occasionally and quietly finish a short story, an essay or a poem, and I always looked forward to reading what he produced. Over time though, his output wasn't very much, and people didn't really know him as a writer. Terry was much more disciplined and bombastic. He would always be working on a treatment or a script; he was always reworking an earlier story and sketching out something new, and he never declined to tell you all about it if you bumped into him.

We can easily get caught up in the glamour of the arts, become enamoured by the status afforded to those who create. Writing is an art and a craft. If we compare a writer to another trade, a much less glamorous trade like a plumber, we would consider someone to be a plumber because eight hours a day they would be working with pipes, fixing leaks and replacing parts. Someone is a plumber because their days are filled with plumbing. No one would call themselves a plumber but spend most of their time taking meetings with dry-wallers and electricians, dreaming up new piping combinations and only once in a while getting their hands dirty (or wet as the case may be). A writer should only call themselves a writer when they spend a good chunk of their day writing. They have to be equal parts tradesperson and artist.

Going back to my two writer friends, Peter was 90% artist and only 10% tradesperson. What he produced was brilliant, but he rarely produced. Terry was completely the opposite. He spent endless hours at his computer writing, rewriting, working out his ideas and promoting his activities. One focused on inspiration, the other on perspiration (and communication).

Over time, Terry got further ahead in his career; he got his scripts produced and generated interest that Peter never did. It kind of broke my heart; I would often be that voice pushing Peter to get his ass in the writer's chair and produce, but he rarely did.

Peter was complacent about his talents, and it seemed like he wasted a lot of his time waiting for inspiration to knock at his door with flowers and chocolates. Terry kept working at it (and working at it). Over time, he developed the ability to produce (though truth be told the quality of his output was never very good) and generate interest in his writing.

—

At work, a similar dynamic is posting targets and strategies with deadlines for deliverables. When I started at

Brightside, there was a strategic plan in place and the management team discussed it frequently. It had pieces of work outlined, named the person accountable for each piece, dates of deadlines and percentage of the work complete. All good. After I had been at the organization for a few months I mentioned the strat-plan to an employee and got a blank stare in return. She had never seen it. It had never occurred to me to ask whether the plan was shared with all staff, I just assumed it had been.

That five-year plan was almost complete so when we drafted a new plan I made sure we rolled it out to all staff. We ran sessions going over the plan, we distributed the full version that the board approved as well as a simplified plan-on-a-page. We held further sessions of dialogue with staff to talk to one another about what in the plan excited them, what they needed clarity about and ideas they had for implementation.

I wondered why the previous plan was not be distributed to all staff. I wondered if it was the same dynamic of putting a note on the fridge (or not, as in this case). Staff can't hold management accountable if they don't know what's expected of us by the board. I see management as a two-way street. We hold staff accountable to do their work and act in a professional and productive way and staff should hold us accountable for following through on our commitments to them and the organization.

Writing a book while working as an executive can feel like one more thing on top of a ton of reading, meeting, writing and working. On those weekends when I was tired and had finished up a very demanding week at work, all I wanted was some downtime. It would have been far easier to postpone my deadline by another week, so much easier to just put it all off. At those times, it was my public declaration that gave me the energy and focus to pull out the iPad and get to work. There's nothing like the disappointment of others to light a fire under you to get your productivity and drive going.

It helps with motivation and to prevent procrastination to publicly declare your intentions. Perhaps it's telling people your ambitions about what role you aspire to. Maybe it's making your intentions known about a project you want to work on or lead. Or telling people about a launch date of a project you worry will slip but you really want everyone focused on achieving it. Use disclosure and transparency to create pressure to ensure you do what you say you're going to do.

—

Eliciting great performances.

An actor needs a good director to help them make the right choices. If the actor's performance isn't believable, they have nothing to hide behind. It is them on the stage or screen looking like they're faking it. They fly without a net. Watching an actor "get" a character and start to step into someone else's shoes, inhabit another persona and become a character from the page is an amazing thing to witness and participate in.

When an actor finds a director they connect with, they will stick with them and continue working with them play after play, film after film. And *vice versa*, a director who finds their onscreen persona, someone who becomes the reality that has, up until that point, only been real inside their heads, is a magical thing. It's why you see certain actors and directors team up in film after film over many years. There is an unspoken bond that forms, a bond that just *is*, and cannot be explained or truly understood.

There are so many wonderful aspects to working on a film: capturing a scene so the audience sees what the director sees in her head, cutting the different shots together in the editing room so the pacing and timing are just right, working with a producer who can solve problems and relieve the constant, immense pressure that is distracting from the creative work at hand. All of these aspects are exciting and even addictive, but none of them compares to the connection between a director and the actors.

One of my greatest joys making films, and one of the only aspects of filmmaking I truly miss, is working with actors. Those neurotic, sensitive, talented, intuitive, vulnerable, opinionated, smart people who, using only their bodies and voices, transport us into a hyper-real, make-believe place where we can suspend our disbelief and absorb lessons in a way like no other. Painters use paints and brushes, writers use keyboards and pencils, sculptors use chisels and stone, musicians play their guitars and trumpets. Actors, however, have no tools with which to express their art, they only have their own selves—their faces, their voices, and their bodies.

Nothing stretched me more as a director than working with actors. They could be challenging and demanding and therefore sometimes difficult, but learning to work with people like that is a great skill to have. It comes in handy all the time.

One of the key things I learned from working with actors is that no two actors like to work in the same way. Some like line readings, some hate them. Some like long philosophical discussions about the meaning of a script, some consider it pretentious. Some want to understand every nuance of a character and their backstory and will research similar people and keep notebooks full of musings about all the things that inform their choices playing that character. Others are the class clowns on set, gobbling up all the attention and entertaining the cast and crew while they wait for the next shot. Some play a version of themselves in every movie. Others are work-horses who come to set every day, are total pros and get it done, take after take, scene after scene, day after day, until the shooting is done and they move on to the next project.

In any given scene, you will have two, three or more actors, each with their own method of getting into their character. Each wanting something a little different from you as the director, all at the same time in the same scene. It's a ton of fun, exhilarating and exhausting, like doing gymnastics while juggling. It stretches you, keeps you limber, and focused.

Good directors, the ones who love working with actors, will balance it all, because they want to coax and elicit the best performance. After all, that's why they cast them in the first place.

Working with actors is a heightened and extreme form of working with professionals in a corporate workplace. We all have our preferred methods of working. We all want a great boss who cares as much about our backstory as we do. Some people like to discuss the "whys" and "hows" of business decisions, and others just want to show up and get the work done.

—

Leading an organization through a global pandemic where people's work situations changed dramatically, suddenly and in ways they had no say over, was a huge challenge. Brightside has an informal and very personal culture. Similar to many not-for-profits, co-operatives and values-based businesses, employees find great value in their connection with their colleagues. The pandemic had many impacts on us, but one that became obvious while we were working from home, was a diminishment of trust and cohesion. As an aside, when I say *working from home*, I am being generous. For much of that time, people were not so much working from home as trying to get some work done while sheltering in place during a global pandemic. That is a very different scenario.

The leadership team was concerned about the amount of assumptions and ascribing of motives we were seeing starting to creep into our culture. In an attempt to name the dynamic, we came up with something we called the three Ps. We would all strive to be: Professional, Productive and Part of the solution.

When staff would raise their concerns, suggestions or complaints, we would focus them on being professional (not personal), productive (does this conversation move dialogue forward?) and part of the solution (are they in this discussion to bitch or because they have ideas for solving the issue?). We added a fourth one at the top, Pause. Before you have the conversation or allow frustration to build, take a pause and reflect to gain perspective. I guess that could be a fifth P: Perspective. Think about this issue from the perspective of other people.

I can't say the three (or four? or five?) Ps solved everything, but they gave us a shared framework and common language to calm things down when the world was confusing and out of control.

In the end, we all want to be treated with respect. If an actor is phoning it in, I don't want to ignore them or overlook their flaws; I am immediately curious as to what's going on and what we can do to pump up the performance. I don't see a lot of that curiosity amongst leaders in the corporate environment. A lot of managers see their staff as gobbling up a bunch of their time—time they don't have enough of.

Like the actor, if a staff-member is phoning in their work, we should help them with their performance. We are quick to judge, quick to assign blame or ascribe motives to other people. Taking the time to bring up the issue at hand and asking a staff-member what's going on is a courageous, albeit necessary, thing to do.

—

Early on in my corporate leadership journey, I performed an assessment of strengths and preferences of the whole team. We each had colours symbolizing what kind of work we preferred. Yellow indicated you were social, creative and expressive. Red indicated you were competitive, determined and strong-willed. Green indicated you were sharing, caring and patient. Blue indicated you were cautious, precise and deliberate.

I found that this simple exercise produced a document that summed me up with stunning accuracy. I am Yellow-Red-Green-Blue, with a ton of yellow, a healthy amount of red and green, and almost no blue.

I had a staff-member at the time whom I really liked when we spoke about matters outside of work, but in meetings I found her to be petty, slow and negative. One day she was in my office discussing a project the team was working on, driving me mad, nitpicking details I wasn't all that focused on. Before leaving, she pointed at my colours, stacked like lego bricks on my desk and almost as an aside she said "Hmmm, I have the exact opposite colours as you." She was Blue-Green-Red-Yellow, with quite a lot of blue and very little yellow.

I looked at her and thought back to my work with actors and realized what I had perceived as petty and negative was her working through issues in a much more methodical way than I do. When I dug deeper, I realized that I led the team from my yellow-biased perspective. I handed out materials in the meeting rather than in advance, expected good dialogue off the cuff, and for everyone to process information in the same way that I do. For this person on my team, that would never work.

She needed materials ahead of time; she needed to absorb and digest them in order to have thoughtful discussion. I had perceived her as slow, when in fact she was thorough and detailed. I perceived her as negative, but she saw risks that I, in my yellow way, was prone to overlooking or discounting. Our working relationship started changing immediately, and I came to see her characteristics that I had previously found bothersome as a strength, and I relied on her perspective to balance out my own.

That conversation, that throw-away comment about our colours was an immense gift. I learned from that conversation that I needed to treat her less like an obstacle to moving forward quickly and more like an actor whose way of working was very different from my own. That different working style evoked a very good final performance, which was nuanced and added a lot to the team.

It also struck me that this was a case for having more creative leaders in organizations. Vancity, as a credit union, had many "blue" people: people who were attracted to banking and finance and loved the details and the spreadsheets. I think my leadership qualities stood out because of the rare "yellow" energy I brought into the organization. I think encouraging different leadership styles is a form of diversity of thought that strengthens an organization. I often found myself playing the friendly contrarian in meetings and I think the discussions and debates that followed made the work better than if a table full of "blue" energy people had been the only people around.

Each day is a unique and different blend of aspirations and anxieties. We all work with multiple people every day who have their own strengths and weaknesses, distresses and successes, worries and resilience. People have challenges in their home lives and specific career aspirations. For the most part, people leave their problems at the door and come to work to contribute what they can. Yet, at times we all come to work with issues we can't ignore, and have things that we are excited about, things that make us nervous, situations we are dealing with, health issues we may be facing. We are like that troupe of actors each trying to work through a scene in our own way. The more we recognize individuality, and embrace the unique contribution each of us brings, the better we will all be able to work together and excel.

We need to take the whole person into consideration as we deal with our peers, bosses and direct reports, to work with them constructively, and perhaps coach and help to manage their performance. Like working with a cast of actors, our job is to learn to work with each of our staff members in the way they want to be worked with. Adapt our style to suit others (without crossing a line where you betray your own overarching style). Find that balance, and you will become a great boss—a coach, mentor and leader. Staff will seek you out and you will have the best employees in your company drawn to work with you.

—

Choosing the music.

Something that's been a constant for me, from my early days in theatre, through my filmmaking career, my dozen years working in web and digital production in and beyond the early dot.com days, is that I love working with creative and technical people to solve problems.

In theatre, it was working alongside lighting and set designers, and writers and actors. In film, it was working with gaffers, lighting technicians, sound production people, and camera operators alongside the actors, editors, musicians, and cinematographers (I named my production company *Group Effort Productions* as a nod to this collaborative spirit.) In digital, it was working with coders and developers, and graphic and user experience designers who made a project exciting. Working with all sorts of people with different skills, backgrounds, and perspectives is certainly going to contribute to a better result than if everyone sees things the same way.

—

We are more focused on diversity and inclusion in the workplace today. Filmmaking gets a bad rap in that regard, as it has historically been such a white and male-dominated industry. As I have matured, I have started to understand how privilege has played a role in my success and advancement. But when I was making films, I didn't think about the role that race, gender, sexual orientation or ability played in who got ahead and who didn't. The concepts of diversity, inclusivity, equity, justice, and belonging simply didn't enter my frame of reference. It was a white man's game and I was a white man so I wasn't really forced to grapple with who was (or wasn't) getting their scripts looked at, getting (or not getting) a lead role, or sitting (or not sitting) in the director's chair.

It is only very recently, since the murder of George Floyd that I have come to understand how white supremacy underpins our society. I reflect on this a lot and realize that just like fish can't see water and humans can't see air, white people won't see the role that white supremacy plays in our world unless we become very intentional about looking for it. The incredible thing is that once I learned to see it, I saw signs of it everywhere. It has played a huge role in my life, giving me advantages in ways I was able to remain blissfully ignorant about. This new understanding of the way our society works is powerful and overwhelming and is part of my life-long journey to learn and improve and do better.

—

If we want to create the best film, and produce the very best product, we need to hire people who have experiences that are different from ours. I, for one, don't know how to light a scene, operate a camera, or compose a musical score. I need to work with people who possess skills and abilities I simply don't have.

It is an amazing and rare thing to bring the art and craft together and meld those practices to make something useful and beautiful. I delight at working with so many different kinds of talented people in the filmmaking process, and none more so than the composers and musicians who write and perform music for films.

At the point when musicians enter the production, all of the footage has been edited and the film has the pacing needed to tell the story. The composer and musicians add texture to the film to heighten the drama, punctuate the emotions, and ultimately make the film more compelling. The cross-disciplinary nature of different kinds of artists working together on a single project is inspiring and satisfying.

When I dreamed up my short film *CheckMating*, the concept of the film and the idea of the music both came to me packaged neatly together. *CheckMating* is about a woman who tests her dates by playing chess with them. Although I wrote dialogue in initial drafts of the script, nothing I came up with captured the romantic and introspective mood I imagined. I always pictured the film with a jazz soundtrack, emphasizing the melody of *Strangers In The Night* which rang through my head on a bus ride to work when the concept of the film came to me in an almost stereotypical flash of inspiration (although we incorporated *Strangers In The Night* into the opening of the score, it had to be removed for legal reasons).

I worked with a jazz trio on a series of musical themes, a different one for each of the protagonist's chess opponents. Ultimately, I scrapped all the dialogue and made a silent film because it occurred to me that music could communicate the tone of each date more effectively and honestly than anything the characters could say. The music allowed me to make a bold creative choice; I took the risk of making a film with no dialogue, where the film's meaning was communicated only through close-up glances and subtle musical cues.

Working with the musicians in a recording studio while the film played on a big screen behind them, bringing all of our different talents together to record the soundtrack, is one of my most cherished memories from filmmaking.

Watching people perform at their best, together, is something I love because it brings out the humanity in any kind of workplace, creative or corporate. Building trust with and among colleagues develops our mutual and unique strengths.

Someone with a very different background and lived experience than I have will focus on a problem differently than I do and will provide a much richer solution to a challenge we face than a bunch of 'me's. Filmmaking provided me with a diverse background, and it extends to the way I lead today. I want to work with people who will challenge me and provide insights and perspectives I never would have imagined. This is true on a film set and it's true in the workplace.

—

When I joined Brightside, we had a very white board of directors. Our mandate is to provide affordable housing across the city, and to best serve our residents we needed people on the board with different experiences and backgrounds. We knew we needed to bring perspectives that we weren't hearing.

The reality in Canada, as it is in many places, is that people who struggle to obtain affordable housing are much more likely to be Black, Indigenous or People of Colour. They are more likely to be disabled or from the LGBTQ+ community. They are more likely to be immigrants or refugees. These are the people Brightside serves; these are the people for whom I am proud to provide homes. And yet the board was mostly straight, middle-class white people. That was a massive disconnect.

We looked at our bylaws and learned that even though we had been a board of nine people for as long as anyone could remember, we were actually able to accommodate a board of between eight and twelve people. We knew that if we stayed at nine people and replaced members every year or two as people left, it would take a decade to bring in the perspectives and diversity we wanted. So we decided to expand the board all the way to twelve members at once. We recruited specifically for the skills we needed, but also for diversity.

By bringing on several people at once we were able to immediately increase the racial diversity of the board, and create gender equity for the first time in our organization's history.

We still have a long way to go to ensure that we bring Indigenous perspectives onto our board. As a land-based organization operating in the unceded territory of the Musqueam, Squamish and Tsleil-Waututh people, who have lived on this land since time immemorial, we have a lot of work to do to reconcile with Canada's colonial history and take steps towards creating equity and justice. When I say land-based, I am considering that Brightside owns and operates 25 properties on land that was never allocated to settlers via treaties with the Indigenous people who lived here long before Europeans showed up. As an organization focused on affordable housing, we are deeply privileged to manage a quarter of a billion dollars worth of property on land that was essentially stolen. It is our job to grapple with that tension and inherent injustice.

This is what real diversity enables. The recognition that a significant disparity or imbalance drives poor decisions. And a board that is 80% white is definitely imbalanced.

Working with people from different backgrounds and with different experiences will challenge the way you work, how you perceive situations and how you approach problems. These insights, if you're open to them, will expand your field of view and make you a stronger leader and thinker. It may increase your empathy. It may give you feedback as a leader that you've never heard before—feedback that may challenge blind spots others have never pointed out.

There is a saying among diversity and inclusion practitioners: Diversity is inviting someone different to the dance, and inclusion is asking that person to dance. I like that. But I don't think it goes far enough.

An important part of bringing someone from a different culture to the board table is learning from one another. Inviting someone who comes from an Indigenous background to join a board and then expecting them to follow the rules of governance established by settler society is insufficient, potentially insulting, and works against the very notion of true inclusion. A board who wants to bring different perspectives to the table and learn from those differences should work to change some of the dynamics and embrace how different cultures govern themselves. That may mean embracing consensus decision-making rather than majority rule. It may mean introducing social interactions to build trust rather than just focusing on business only. It may mean shifting the time and place of the meetings, or offering child care.

So if diversity is inviting someone different to the dance, and inclusion is inviting that person to dance, I would suggest true justice is inviting them to select some of the music we all dance to.

As I write this, we are revising our governance bylaws at Brightside to reserve at least one spot at our board table for someone with an Indigenous perspective. As a land-owning organization, we feel this is a critical step towards confronting the injustices of colonialism and ensure that our future includes righting some of the many wrongs imposed upon the First Nations, Inuit and Métis peoples in Canada. I assume that this journey will not be straightforward. Mistakes will happen, insensitive comments will be made, awkward moments will definitely ensue. We will never grow if we don't get uncomfortable. We may need to manage conflict so that it is productive and leads to greater understanding. We can't improve if we don't learn and unlearn, and some of that evolution will be challenging. We are still in the early days of this journey at Brightside, so time will tell. I am hopeful.

Seeking different ways of operating that honours different perspectives and can withstand disagreement and changing how things have always been done is imperative. Creativity and stagnation are natural enemies. We can try to avoid new perspectives or new ways of doing things because they are unfamiliar and we might make mistakes. Or we can find the courage to embrace new things and not feel ashamed if we get it wrong.

Good work doesn't come from groupthink. Everyone has their own style, and, like the filmmaker collaborating with musicians, everyone approaches their work a little differently. We will benefit from a team with diverse experiences and opinions. Understand those differences in your team and embrace them.

—

Get used to failing.

No one would imagine a film set as a place where people aren't allowed to take risks. In any creative venture, there is an expectation that some choices aren't going to work out. If I was on set with a fear of failure, I would need to get every shot perfect on the first take, for every shot to be used in the scene and for every scene to be kept in the final edit. There's no way to get to a finished product that is original and interesting, without going in some wrong directions and needing to redo some takes, rewrite a scene or change the ending.

Stories of actors doing twenty-one takes to get a scene right, or a director and cinematographer taking a week to get a complex shot just perfect, are legendary in the film business. In fact, the very notion of the cutting room floor comes from the film business—a metaphor used to demonstrate work we will cut out for the sake of effectiveness, brevity and clarity.

We're all focused on innovating—at times, so much so that I worry the word has lost a lot of meaning. Innovation, when you boil it down, can simply be defined as seeing your work as a creative pursuit. I assume anyone curious enough about this topic to be reading this book would see their work in this context, as a series of creative endeavours meant to drive results, outcomes and outputs.

Some imagine creativity as chaotic. Many people think of the process of painting and imagine paints and brushes everywhere, or musicians rehearsing and imagine a noisy, messy, smoke-stained studio, with beer cans underfoot. Creativity, however, doesn't imply a lack of discipline. Most people would see a film set as a place that is inherently creative—a place where risks are taken. Yet, a film set in so many ways is similar to a military operation with all the different moving parts marching towards a common goal. It is a place that is seeking both creativity and order.

That balance of looseness and precision is optimized if the filmmaker knows what they're doing. If they choose the right script, hire the right crew, cast the right actors and have a true sense of purpose about the film, they will radically increase their chances for success.

—

Once the elements of your career are in place for success—you're working at a company where you feel a good fit, for someone you trust, and with a team you believe in—your job is to create a safe environment where people can take risks. I know I'd rather work in an environment where risks and failure are permitted and even expected.

I encounter many people who are afraid to take risks, afraid of failure in the workplace. Over the last several years, we've become better at talking about the concept of failure at work, but haven't really moved the bar in actually tolerating failure.

I find the way we talk about failure in the workplace to be odd and counter-productive. Traditional large companies and bureaucracies tend to refuse to acknowledge that failure ever happens, while modern companies, especially technology companies, put a ton of focus and emphasis on failure, even to the point of celebrating it. Staff at tech firms are encouraged to bring forward examples of when they failed as a way of demystifying people's fear of failure.

In the world of film, no one shows up on set excited to fail or ready to share their latest failure story. We simply acknowledge that you can't produce a film without some failure — we neither fetishize and celebrate it, nor hide from it and cover it up. We strive to create something great amidst the occasional but inevitable blunders. A boom mic enters shot, a nearby siren ruins the sound recording, an actor flubs a line or a camera movement is jittery. So many opportunities for failure. My job is to handle these things with nuance, refocus, and help people feel like those moments are no big deal.

Focusing on failure, to me, is a little like focusing on meetings. They happen as part of the process. We don't talk all that much about embracing meetings (although maybe we should, given the ease with which people set up meetings that are often unnecessary, too long and over-attended). Meetings are a tool to move work forward and to ensure clarity amongst a team. We don't get into business in order to have meetings, we have meetings in order to do business. Failure is similar. We shouldn't glorify failure, nor should we hide from it. As humans, we will stumble. The faster we can brush ourselves off and move forward, the better. If a leader unintentionally (or intentionally) creates a sense of shame from a failure, then people will be afraid to act, because as humans, to act means sometimes to fail.

There are times, however, when failure does warrant a closer look. My job as a director was to see if the same mistakes were occurring over and over again. If the boom mic was continuously entering frame, or if an actor was constantly messing up their lines, or if bills weren't getting paid on time, I would discuss it with the person making that mistake. I'd get the boom operator and the camera operator together to figure out why it was happening. I'd take the actor aside and draw on my empathy to find out why they were struggling with the dialogue. I'd ask the production people why cheques were going out late.

If the same mistake continued to be made time and time again, perhaps there was a gap in knowledge or competence and we needed to get that person some training or move them to a different role. If the situation couldn't be rectified, I may have a mature conversation with them about finding a better fit in another role or at another organization. In the worst case, I may have to remove them from the team. I did that assessment quietly, because people can't perform well under a constant fear of failure or the threat of losing their job. They need a safe environment to work.

I've worked at places where people were chronically afraid of the hammer coming down. There were layoffs happening for reasons people couldn't see. I don't like to fire people and create an environment of fear and stress in the office.

When a leader has tried everything possible to rectify a situation and feels that there is no choice but to remove someone from the organization, in my experience it always works out for the best. I've overseen many dismissals over the years and can't think of a time when a firing didn't result in someone finding a better situation. What I have witnessed is that it isn't the firing itself that causes issues in the workplace or for a team, but the ramifications of not dealing with someone who is causing issues. I learned an important aphorism from a trusted colleague: Hire slowly, fire quickly. The cost of not firing someone when it is warranted is high, and payment takes the form of increased toxicity, low engagement, and lack of trust and cohesion.

The shock of getting fired stings. It can sometimes take a while for someone to bounce back and find the right job. But over time, people almost always end up better off, and usually happier than they were before they were fired. That difficult experience leads them to make a shift, and it was perhaps their reluctance to make a needed shift that caused their performance to suffer, their attitude to calcify, or behaviour to become problematic.

—

In so many ways, a background in film is an excellent leaping-off point for a career in business. I got used to small "failures" all the time, understood they were part of the process, looked to find patterns that indicated something more serious was going on and helped people get to a sense of collaborative co-creation. I instilled a sense of pride and ease to help everyone improve their own feeling of contributing to something greater. I developed a leadership style that included humour, empathy, curiosity and a sense of camaraderie to create a trusting work environment, even if I felt stressed and frustrated. The last thing I wanted was to over-react to issues or have others panic. No one can feel safe in that kind of pressured environment. If I don't manage my own frustration, people will choke. Actors will start making mistakes, someone will leave a coffee cup in shot or a costume will get damaged.

When I joined Brightside, there were four major real estate redevelopment projects in the very early planning stage. Four of the buildings that had reached their end of life were being redeveloped to create many more modern, comfortable and environmentally sustainable homes for people with limited means in North America's least affordable city. The projects were getting rolling, and there were many gaps in our knowledge. A more risk-averse organization would have stopped to answer these questions before taking further steps. Staff may have felt stressed out by all the uncertainty and unknowns. I felt right at home. I knew the organization was a good match for me because everyone from the volunteer board of directors through the management team and across the entire staff wanted to keep moving. They were unified by a deep sense of purpose to create more affordable housing for their fellow Vancouverites and could work through the unknowns as they went.

This sense of purpose allowed us to answer questions while driving the projects forward. There were some scary times, such as when we didn't know if essential government financing would come through. We were out way over our skis. But that entrepreneurial attitude was pervasive, and my background allowed me to keep people feeling safe while undertaking significant but intentional risks.

That smart risk-taking paid off as project after project received the grants, financing and approvals that we required. I am sure that the team's willingness to fail in pursuit of greater success conveyed a sense of confidence that attracted external stakeholders and partners and helped us to succeed. People were on our side.

You have to have a sense of purpose about the project you're working on. Like making a film, you have to be confident that you chose your script well, have a great cast and crew around you, and that you have connected them to the purpose of the story. If you can create that sense of purpose and camaraderie and communicate it effectively, then everything will come together. You will have nurtured an environment where risks can be taken and failures can happen in pursuit of something of value. If all those elements are in place, then enough of the risks you and your team will take will be successful, and innovation — whether incremental or revolutionary — will result.

—

Killed with a fork.

A lot of companies do ice breakers before meetings to loosen everyone up, help people connect and get to know each other to create a more comfortable and productive work environment. I find these are especially good before any meeting in which deep thinking and creativity are needed.

The ice breakers tend to be things like: Let's go around the table and say who you are, how long you've worked here and name the first concert you ever attended (mine was The Police at the Pacific Coliseum in 1983). A good ice breaker is short and should include an activity that is very specific. An ice breaker wouldn't be successful if people had to go around the room and say their name, how long they've worked at the organization and then say anything, anything at all that they want. People would be stopped in their tracks, paralyzed, not knowing where to begin.

When I graduated from high school, I wanted to start making films and writing plays, and showcasing them for the public. I was entrepreneurial. I didn't want to wait until someone gave me an opportunity, I wanted to create my own opportunities. One night, over many hours of coffee at a late night diner, two friends who were also aspiring writers and I decided to put on an evening of one-act plays. We wanted to do it ourselves. We didn't want to wait for the opportunity; at 21 years old, we decided to write the plays, rent a theatre, promote the evening and just do it.

But wait, where should we begin?

If you were tasked with writing a one-act play about anything at all, no barriers, no constraints, your brain might freeze. Write about anything, anything at all? The mind goes blank.

We needed a concept to get us started. A device that would have enough latitude that we could be creative in our approach, but contained enough specificity that it would start our creative juices flowing. Luckily, that night, over those steaming cappuccinos, we struck the concept: In each of our plays, at some point someone had to be killed with a fork. We called the evening of plays *Killed With A Fork*. We had something intriguing, with enough of a hook that we could have fun with it, and yet broad enough that we weren't at all concerned that the plays would be too similar to each other.

At the time, we each lived in a different city, so we decided that on a specific date, two months in the future, we would mail the scripts to the other two (this was 1989, a little bit before email). We left the cafe that night and each went back to our home city, eager to start writing and get one step closer to producing our evening of one-act plays. Awesome.

Two months later, as agreed, we each mailed copies of our finished script to the others, wondering what we would receive in return. When I got the other scripts in the mail, I was delighted that we had three totally different one-act plays; I was filled with joy, albeit dark joy, flipping through the pages in anticipation of how and when a character would be killed with a fork (in one, someone was killed with a pitchfork, but close enough).

It was an excellent hook, and that one limitation opened so much creativity. Creativity that otherwise would not have been tapped, as we would struggle with where to start, what to write, wondering whether our play would work with the other two. The concept of needing to write a play in which someone would get killed with a fork was just enough to get ideas flowing and start us down a path towards productivity.

The same is true of business innovation. Tell a team to go be innovative, and you're probably looking at a lot of wasted time. Even if you have a limitation, is it specific enough? I've seen groups of people in various innovation pods spin their wheels for weeks because the question they're tackling is too broad. If you don't know where you're going, any path will get you there.

I often tell these teams to add a limitation. If they're looking at an innovative banking product for youth, add in the concept of forced savings. Or focus on a specific youth segment, like those just graduating from university and their specific needs. Add in one limitation, and if ideas don't start, either change that limitation, or add one more. Sometimes working your way into a tight box can help you think of a very specific innovation to escape that box in a way no one else has.

The current explosion of digital solutions comes from founders seeking to address one problem that one market segment faces. If they can tackle that one problem they can move on from there, building solutions on top of each other.

Innovation is unlocked because creative leaders will be looking at the problem uniquely and with great specificity. Entrepreneurs and intrapreneurs both want that one *Killed With a Fork* kind of breakthrough to drive progress, increase productivity and get greater results.

—

Mission is everything.

When I was deep in pre-production on my first and only feature film, *The Engagement Party*, I got a call one day from my landlord, Rob. Rob was a great guy and a very good landlord. Although he didn't do a ton of maintenance on the duplex in the Green Lake area of Seattle where my wife and I lived, he was nice and kept our rent super low. Low rent was essential in those filmmaking days, as my salary fluctuated widely, and not infrequently down to zero.

Rob called me one day and asked if everything was okay. It was unusual for him to call, and it turned out that I had missed paying rent for the first time in several years of being his tenant. I was very embarrassed, and told Rob that I was elbow deep in making a feature film, that I had totally spaced out and would mail him a cheque immediately. Rob started asking about the film, what it was and why it had taken over my life.

We talked about the film for several minutes and I shared my very personal reasons why the project was important to me. It was a very different pitch than I would give to investors or people in the film business. It was just me telling someone I knew why I was making the film. In fact, looking back, my embarrassment over missing a regular rent payment probably made me want to convince him why the film was so all-consuming, and that I wasn't a flake who forgot to pay rent for no reason.

I was conveying to Rob the mission of the film. Not the story the film told, although I'm sure I touched on that. I didn't describe the breakdown of costs, or when we would shoot the film or where the locations were. I didn't get into who was involved and which local actors were being cast. I told him why the film was of such importance to me that I forgot to pay my rent.

Some of you may have guessed what happened next, which makes you smarter than me, because I was shocked—absolutely stunned by what he did. He invested in my film. I had turned a call from my landlord over a missed rent payment into him investing far more money than my monthly rent into my film—without reading my investor materials and without seeing the script treatment (both of which I sent to him after the call). He invested in me and my passion.

When I made films, they were incredibly low-budget productions. I was good at negotiating huge discounts, or even free equipment and services. I did this by connecting with people I was negotiating with, telling them about the film I was making, and why it was important to me. As an example, my short film *CheckMating* was originally budgeted at $12,000, and I was able to make it for a mere $1,800. I didn't have to pay for a camera rental, lighting, film stock, film lab processing, editing equipment, or much of anything. Food on set and film festival applications were my biggest line-items. Everything else, by focusing on why I wanted to make the film and sharing my passion, was offered to me at huge discounts, and often for free.

—

Fast forward a few years, and my wife Amy and I were living a very good life in Los Angeles. A year after moving there, however, we started to realize that LA was not going to be our forever home, and we started to feel a strong pull to move back to my hometown of Vancouver, Canada. We talked about what we liked about LA, and about what we missed that we wish it had.

By the end of that conversation, walking along Venice Beach, we had decided something very profound. Something that would define the rest of our lives. We realized that we needed to live a life that when we told someone about aspects of our lives, we would actually be describing our personal values.

Our main issue with life in LA was that we just didn't feel like us. As we pondered the feeling that we didn't fit in as we walked across the warm sand, we realized what we wanted. We wanted to live a life in which our values played a central role. We felt stuck because we wanted our values to be demonstrated in our lifestyle choices, by the decisions we made every day.

What do I mean by living our values? I'm talking about how long our commute was, the environmental impact of our daily lives, what the fruits of our labour ultimately supported, the ability to shop at local companies, how often we saw our friends. Even what kind of car we drove and how many cars we owned. All of those choices, big and small, felt disconnected from what was truly important to us.

Our move back to Vancouver was a *mission* move, a move about living our values. That's how we decided to live in a very community-oriented neighbourhood called Commercial Drive, full of independent shops and businesses. We focused on shopping locally whenever possible, we gave up our second car and only had an electric-hybrid between us, and I joined a local carshare co-operative, where I would later be elected chair of the board of directors.

This key pivot-point in our lives was about understanding ourselves and acting upon that understanding. As leaders, if we are to be great bosses, coaches, mentors and peers we have to work on our emotional intelligence and self-awareness. We have to continuously strive to improve as people—that's part of the work that few people talk about.

Eventually, once I got settled and had enough of working for digital agencies or large publicly-traded companies, I left a permanent job at a large Telco for a three-month contract at Vancity, Canada's largest community credit union. My values and the values of my employer matched up perfectly for the first time in my life.

Before Vancity, I job-hopped a lot. I once had a recruiter tell me that my resume was both very attractive and very scary. Attractive because I had so many work experiences with well-known clients. Over my many gigs I had worked with clients like Honda, Nike, Disney, 20th Century Fox, Intuit and Universal Pictures. But scary because I had lots of stints at companies ranging from 12 to 18 months; bringing me on board and investing in my training felt like a risk, because I was unlikely to stick around for even a couple of years.

I began to wonder if I lacked some sense of commitment or stick-with-it-ness that I needed. Why so many short stints? I knew that I just hadn't found the right place where I felt a sense of commitment and reciprocity. A place that matched my values. Before Vancity I had never even thought about the values of the companies I worked for. I had never worked at a company that even spoke about its values. I think back to my former employers, and I have absolutely no idea what any of those companies' values were.

My initial three-month contract at Vancity went well. It was a good mutual fit and after my contract got extended, I became permanent and over time received promotions and different lateral assignments. By the time I left I had been there just shy of 14 years. That's an order of magnitude longer than I had worked anywhere else in my life (I think I worked at a motion picture lab in Seattle for three years, which had been my longest gig). I emerged as a leader at Vancity because I knew precisely why I worked there and felt an alignment with the mission deep in my bones. I knew the answer to the question: *Why me, why this role, why now?* The organization's purpose encouraged me to improve as a person, and those improvements made me a better leader.

—

Good, well-intentioned people can make bad films. That's because filmmaking is complex, and there are lots of choices and compromises to make; sometimes things just don't work out. If a director knowingly starts a film with a script they think is subpar or with a team that doesn't have the skills to do their jobs with excellence then they have just significantly reduced their likelihood of success.

If you want to thrive as a leader, it's important to work for a company whose mission you love and understand, a company you couldn't *not* work for, and with a team whose success you are driving for both personally and collectively. From that position of strength you then need to develop self-awareness and emotional intelligence. That's easier said than done, for sure, but that's the goal. If you know that goal isn't being met, be on the lookout for new scripts and change companies as soon as you possibly can.

Now at Brightside, I know that I could never work at an organization where I don't believe in the mission and align with the values. I've become a bit of a values snob and seeing the connection between what I do for a living and a larger societal benefit is completely central to my approach to work. That's the clarity my wife and I discovered that day on Venice Beach.

I think of my landlord Rob now and then, about that great little duplex near Green Lake when our costs were low, our incomes were tiny, and I had the freedom to pursue filmmaking. I think about what that phone conversation must have been like for Rob, calling me to collect on a late rent payment only to hear about a film project and feel inspired enough that he decided to invest. It boggles my mind to this day and taught me a lesson that was infinitely more valuable than the cheque he wrote to me. He didn't really invest in my film, he invested in me, and that was the first time someone had taken such an interest in my dreams and ambitions. That was a powerful moment.

When people know you lead with passion and purpose, they will confide in you, seek your feedback and input, and you will get asked to be their coach and mentor. If you're clear on your own purpose as a leader, you will return that trust with great feedback and input. When you're clear about your values, people want to work with you, for you and to have you on their team. At this point in my career, I could only ever work for an organization steeped in mission, one I truly believe in.

—

The third take rule.

In the chapter *Get Used To Failing* we discussed that to make a film, or embark on any creative endeavour, it is imperative to keep cool and have a sense of humour when things inevitably go off the rails. My attitude towards failure was shaped by my background making films, because so much of the time there are more things that can go wrong than can go right. And there's no way to have one without the other.

Whenever you make a film, you end up breaking down each scene into different shots. Each shot will have multiple takes in which the scene is acted out over and over again until the acting, the lighting, the framing, the camera movement, the background set, everything is just the way the director wants it. That take is usually the one that ends up in the final film.

Sometimes, you get the perfect take the first time, but it usually takes several takes to nail it. I used to notice that it was the third take that would often be the first time that a given shot was captured well. The first take was shaky, and perhaps an actor would flub a line—it was almost like a final rehearsal. The second take would often be slightly worse. Then, the third take would come out really nicely. A flow to the shot emerged, people were increasingly comfortable and everything came together for a successful take.

Most directors, myself certainly included, would say, "Let's try another one for safety, just to make sure we got it." At that point, the scene would fall apart. Takes four and five would be a disaster, and take seven would have the boom mic in shot. The sunk-cost fallacy suggests that at that point, knowing the time and money being spent on set are ratcheting up, the director should say, "You know what, we got that great third take, let's move on." But, they don't; they persevere, and takes eight and nine go by, and the mood starts feeling awkward.

Then, something magical happens. Take eleven would be amazing. There would be something about the performance, the nuance of the camera move combined with a gesture the actor made that was perfect. Awesome, nailed it! The crew would break down the set and get ready for the next shot.

It may have taken two hours longer to get to that perfect eleventh take but, dammit, it was worth the time and money.

Three months later, in the editing room, poring over the shots to assemble a rough cut of the whole scene, I would look at take three and take eleven, the perfectly good take and the perfectly magical take, and honestly, I couldn't tell the difference. They were both good, and the nuance on set that elevated take eleven was insignificant in the cold light of the editing room. When the takes were cut up and intermingled with the other footage to assemble the scene, the two takes were indistinguishable from one another.

As someone who both produced and directed my films, I reflected on the extra two hours of people's time, of daylight passing, of equipment rental costs, of people's patience and goodwill that was spent. And for what? Take three was great; we all should have had the confidence in that, moved along and kept up our momentum.

I reflect on the third and eleventh takes a lot. If I am writing a business case, I don't want to hand in the first draft—the first take—because it will be rough and unpolished and probably miss the mark. At the same time, I have also been guilty of spending far too long on a business case, putting too much in and trying to make it perfect. In doing so, I used too many resources, too many data points, too much of people's time to get to an eleventh draft, when the third draft would have done just fine.

Having said that, there are critical times when that eleventh take is required. In my feature film, *The Engagement Party*, there is a crucial moment of understanding between the two main characters—the couple getting married. The drama of the entire film hinged on a moment between them as they shared deep personal insights and grew to understand each other better. The emotional honesty, the way the camera slowly moved in on their quiet, understated performances, all of that came from repetition, from the ten previous takes exploring the scene and the meaning.

In the editing room, though the differences between the earlier "good enough" third take and that eleventh take were small, they were noticeable and made an impact. The eleventh take in this case had an almost imperceptible emotional honesty that elevated the scene in a way that the film demanded. The film would have suffered without that extra emotional weight and vulnerability at that precise moment. The extra time and effort were worth it.

Part of balancing the third and eleventh take is knowing your audience. Have you met with the stakeholders and those who will approve your business case to find out what they are looking for? Do you know what "good" looks like? Write everything required to get the case approved, certainly don't put in less than that, but, equally important, don't put in more. You can't get extra approval on a project. I don't know of a board of directors that will give you more budget or time than you asked for because your business case was so damn good. You will get the same output from that eleventh take as you would have from the third. In the time and effort spent between those two takes, you have other work piling up that you're not focused on, because you're putting 'A' effort into something where you just need to pass.

If your whole career is riding on a proposal or a project, then spend the extra time, by all means. It will all be worth it to not just cross the finish line, but to soar past it. Know when you need that extra time and effort to get it perfect, and when the difference won't be noticed by your audience. The wisdom to know that the third take nailed it or that you need to persist to the eleventh take comes with experience.

I must add, in business as in life (in fact, much more so than in indie filmmaking), it is often possible to go back and get that other take, and recapture that third-take energy. If that business case or project doesn't pass the stage-gate you are hoping for, in my experience, you usually get good feedback and have another chance to come back with a refined case.

In film, there are reshoots, if you absolutely didn't get what you needed the first time (harder to get, the lower the budget); in business, there are second chances. Know ahead of time if you have one shot to get it right or if you can collect that feedback, refine and re-present.

—

Some executives aim for perfection and want to get everything right all of the time. When I speak to executives who have this perfectionist streak, I am surprised they got as far as they did, expecting *everything* to go right. That isn't having a high standard, it is a mistaken understanding of how life works, how human beings operate. The goal isn't to aim for perfection, which is impossible to achieve.

When I first took on the Director of Web Engagement & Banking role at Vancity, I wrote a strategic plan for all of the upgrades and additions I felt were required to enhance our digital channels to enact the organization's strategic direction. I wanted to find an analogy to the digital work that the executive could relate to and get excited about so they would approve the strategy. At the time, I noticed leaders referred to online banking (still relatively new then) as the "online branch." They related it to the branch experience, which was very familiar to them. I modelled my presentation on that and aligned the funding for the enhancements needed to improve the online experience to the annual budget of a large branch (in this analogy, online banking was by far the largest branch).

I was excited about my presentation, but my strategy was rejected. The organization at the time wasn't ready to invest the amount of money I had proposed into the digital channel. This wasn't a rare occurrence at the time; many of my peers at other institutions faced similar rejections. I refocused my efforts, pulled out the pieces I thought were critical to the users of the site to stay current with industry trends, and went back, not with a full strategy, but with a component approach.

I wanted to take a more holistic approach, but that wasn't successful. Instead I went back and created a new third take, and moved some significant individual business cases forward.

—

The 19th film festival.

I made lots of ultra low-budget short videos in high school and university, but after leaving university, I wanted to make a more significant and professional film. I poured my heart and soul into a film called *Greenwich Meridian*, about an actor struggling to perform a play that brought up painful personal memories he hadn't dealt with. It was a 33-minute 16mm film that I spent all my money on and got family to spend their money on too. It was a huge effort; it took me a good four years from sitting down to start writing the script through finishing the film and having a print I could show others (should a 16mm projector and a big white wall be available).

By the time I was done, I was completely sick of the film. It wasn't as good as I had hoped, I was broke, and I was exhausted from the years of effort while having a day job.

I may have felt like I was done, but that's when the critical promotional phase was just beginning. Now I had to sell the film, promote it, tell everyone about it, try to get press, arrange screenings, and most critically, apply to film festivals—lots and lots of film festivals. Just when I was done living with it 24/7, and could see every bit of it that hadn't turned out as well as the film I saw in my mind, I had to convince others that it was awesome. That is very hard to do.

I submitted *Greenwich Meridian* to eighteen film festivals and got rejected from all of them. Ugh, so disappointing and discouraging.

I asked the festivals for feedback and learned a few things. I learned that I was right. *Greenwich Meridian*'s flaws, the delta between the beautiful, moving film in my mind and what was captured on the 16mm cellulose was a big one. The film just wasn't that great. Digging deeper into the feedback and looking at what did get into the eighteen film festivals I received rejection letters from, I learned where I went wrong. I learned what the short-film adjudicators at film festivals were looking for.

They didn't want half-hour 16mm films. They received lots of them, and they couldn't program many of them. They couldn't put them in front of a feature, because not many people want to sit through a half-hour film and then a 120-minute film back to back. Also, at that time, most feature-length films screened at festivals were projected on 35mm, and they didn't like switching between a 16mm projector and sound system and a 35mm feature on the fly, during an uninterrupted screening (this was before modern digital projection systems).

That was good intel. In addition to my film not being very good, I was making it harder for film festival programmers to plug my film into their lineups. I realized that my 33-minute 16mm film had to be the absolute best in the world for the festival staff to overcome their own operational limitations to add it to their programs.

In my next film *CheckMating*, I took the lessons I had learned to heart, and as a result made a 7-minute 35mm short film that was tailored for what film festival program directors were looking for. The concept and title had come to me in a bit of a stereotypical epiphany on the bus on my way to work one morning. The whole film is told through glances and chess moves between the protagonist—the young woman—and each of her five dates. The film had a beautiful score, and no talking. My choice to go without talking meant that my film could play any film festival in the world without needing subtitles. Another barrier to programming removed.

I had also worked harder than ever as a filmmaker and simply made a much better film. It was a film I never grew sick of. I stayed excited about *CheckMating* from the moment I first dreamt up the idea to the day I screened my first print for colleagues, family and friends in Seattle. My excitement about the concept and the film remained high, and when it was done I was dying to promote it and have people see it.

I started applying to film festivals. It was at that point when I learned a lesson that I will never forget. I was so confident in the film that I applied to festival after festival after festival. I kept money aside for the cost of videotapes (remember 1996?), shipping, and the expense of actual film festival application fees ($25-100 each).

Can you guess what happened next? I got rejected from the first eighteen festivals I applied to—exactly like *Greenwich Meridian*. I was so gutted. I couldn't believe it. Eighteen rejection letters piled up, one on top of the other. This was such a good film, and I was so proud of it. I couldn't do any better than this, and it was made to the exact specifications film festivals were looking for. What the hell was going on?

Because we sometimes need to get hit over the head to learn our lessons, I got into the nineteenth film festival I applied to. The Boston Film Festival. And then I got into another. And another and another and another. *CheckMating* played over 30 film festivals all over the world and started getting invited to festivals without my needing to apply at all. It ended up getting a distributor and was licensed to airlines and TV stations around the globe. Over time, the film actually made money, albeit not very much. Still, I had made a short film that went into the black. It was very, very gratifying.

As an aside, the organizers for one of the film festivals in California I was accepted into were very nice, and invited me to say a few words at the screening. But as a not-for-profit film society, they couldn't afford to fly me down and put me up in a hotel. I remember sitting at home in Seattle, knowing my film was playing at that very moment, and I wasn't there. I did everything I could to manage my budget frugally, but still didn't have enough to attend. I had to prioritize applying to film festivals over attending them, and so I focused on getting my film into festivals even though I couldn't afford to be there in person.

Today I look at my own level of energy and passion I have as a leader, and I reflect on those days of film promotion. Does my energy endure or does it start to waver over time? My own personal commitment needs to remain strong in order to model the behaviours and dedication I want people to see and respond to. I look back and wonder when my love for *Greenwich Meridian* started to wane, and if there was a point at which I should have changed something. Was there something I could have done as a writer or a director on set or in the editing room that could have produced a better product? If my personal resolve had stayed high, would I have had the energy and enthusiasm to promote it like I needed to? Perhaps my commitment would have allowed me to find the money required to apply to more festivals.

We're all busy people, working on a lot of things at once. It's very easy to finish something and immediately move on to the other 89 things we have going on. As a leader, I need to ensure that projects have the funding and resources to go all the way to completion. I need to make sure I have attention and focus for my team and I never make anyone feel like I don't have time for them when they need me. I can't stop applying to film festivals after eighteen rejections if it is going to be the nineteenth that starts success.

We need to ensure that initiatives plan for sustainment once the project is done and perhaps have a line item in the budget for promotion. It's important to focus on key milestones, celebrate accomplishments and communicate the completion of projects. I don't always think about celebrating with staff, it's just not the way I'm wired, but I've learned to ask teams to plan a party when a project is complete, and to communicate the status, outcomes and successes that they achieve.

The lesson from *Greenwich Meridian* could have been that after eighteen rejections from film festivals for *CheckMating*, it was time to call it quits. *CheckMating* would have been another failure. Instead, I listened to my own energy and sense of commitment and personal agency to keep going. As a result, I was able to promote the work and find success.

—

Do your job.

On a film set, there are a lot of different jobs and lots of different people in those jobs. Each job is important in their own way, and each person plays an important role in the making of a film.

There is a great story by celebrated playwright and filmmaker David Mamet in the introduction to his screenplay *House of Games*, where he talks about the experience he had making the film, his first as a director. Theatre and film are both collaborative art forms, but there are key differences in how they are collaborative and in how people best work together to achieve common goals.

In the days before digital capture, film footage had to be shipped to a lab to be processed and printed. That footage was called dailies, because it was all the film printed from the previous day of shooting for the director and key personnel to review. Dailies screenings are exciting. Key people involved with production—usually the cinematographer, the editor and the producer—would sit with the director and only they would be privy to how the film looked and what was being translated to the screen.

As we discussed in the chapter *The Third Take Rule*, when you get a good take of a shot, you would have it printed, and those printed shots would be projected for those select people. The cinematographer would make sure the footage was well lit and the camera movement worked for the mood, and the editor would get a sense of the footage coming into the editing room for rough assembly of scenes. The director would obviously need to see the footage to know how the ingredients of the film were coming together. Usually others aren't invited because, well, we all know what happens when you have too many cooks in the kitchen.

David Mamet, coming from the loose environment of the theatre, described how he invited all sorts of people into the dailies screenings: grips, gaffers, camera operators, actors, you name it. These are people who may have literally never been invited to a screening of dailies before. On top of this unique invitation to attend, the crew would be asked to vote on which takes they liked the best to hand to the editor for inclusion in the cut.

Now, the collaborative side of me says that's amazing — the more the merrier. David Mamet would have people vote on their favourite takes and get their input. Super collaborative. Awesome, right?

It turns out, not so much. After a little while, Mamet realized that he had to stop asking the crew for feedback. Why? People usually like getting asked for their opinion. Well, it turns out, there is a question of accountability at play.

The director's job is simple. It is to make decisions. Lots and lots of decisions. One of those critical decisions is determining which shots will end up going to the editor for their assembly. Gaffers work hard to make sure the lighting looks just the way it should. The gaffer doesn't ask the director to move a light slightly to see whether she likes it better. The gaffer does that and makes those choices on behalf of the entire production.

As much as we like being asked our opinion and to weigh in on decisions, we also want a sense of fairness—a sense that we are each pulling our weight. If you're in management, people need to have confidence in your leadership—your ability to make good decisions and coach or advise others. If a director invites the gaffer into the dailies screening and asks them to vote on scenes, the gaffer may see the director as not being able to make decisions—the most critical part of their job. That act may actually erode trust that the director is qualified or suited for their accountabilities.

Being egalitarian and collaborative is often good, but it is critical to collective success that we know who is accountable (and paid) for different levels of experience and decision-making.

—

When I was first promoted to a senior management role, I had a colleague with whom I worked closely. Lilly and I worked together for quite a while and were excellent colleagues. With my promotion, I was suddenly her boss. That can often be an awkward transition, and given my inexperience as a leader, I didn't handle it well at all.

What I should have done was sit down with Lilly and discuss all the ways our working relationship wouldn't change, but also focus on the ways my becoming her manager would change the dynamics between us. I should have been upfront with her (and myself) about what it would be like for me to manage her.

Instead, we never discussed it, and I couldn't bring myself to manage Lilly effectively. I didn't direct her, I didn't give her feedback or focus on her projects. She worked on what she wanted with less and less direction or input from me. I was just too inexperienced and uncomfortable being her manager.

As a result of my actions (or inactions), her performance suffered. I am not a very hierarchical person; that often serves me well, as I am told by my staff that I'm very approachable and they can tell me what's going on. But through my missteps with Lilly, I learned that hierarchy is important to recognize, even if it isn't drawn on very often. She needed a boss, as we all do.

I left Lilly alone and her work became less relevant. She was eventually let go from the organization in a way that wasn't fair to her and didn't demonstrate her capabilities. Our work friendship ended abruptly and awkwardly.

I think about Lilly from time to time, because I wish I could go back and handle that situation very differently. With my promotion, we should have recognized that we would be playing different roles in the organization and discussed what would change. I could have opened the door to the kind of conversations an employee needs to have with their boss, different from those they have with a direct peer. I let my own insecurities and inexperience get in the way of open dialogue about what had changed between us.

That would have been a different kind of leadership—for me to focus on what we as a business unit needed to achieve while also being empathetic to what was going on for the employee (and for me). By understanding Lilly's perspective, I could have tried harder to engineer a win-win scenario, whether that created a re-engagement for Lilly in the work or created a decision in her that it was time to leave the organization (or some other scenario neither of us could have predicted).

I was trying to be open and egalitarian, like David Mamet did in his dailies screenings. I should have recognized my accountability and stepped into that, and owned it. By not doing that I created confusion and distrust which ended in an employee leaving an organization in a way that wasn't commensurate with her potential or contribution.

—

Living in your car.

"Just because you live in your car, doesn't mean you're going to be famous."

Those were the cruel but honest words spoken from the stage at a panel on filmmaking, by a successful producer to a struggling director in the audience. The aspiring director had raised his hand and warned all who were present that he simply had to make it in the business, that he was incredibly committed to his films—so committed, in fact, that he was living in his car to afford to stay in Los Angeles.

Living in your car may demonstrate commitment, but it may just as easily demonstrate that you have lost all perspective. In creative pursuits there is often a real tension between delusion and persistence.

When I was living in Seattle in the '90s as an independent filmmaker, social media was still a decade from springing to life. As a result, when I left Seattle, I lost touch with some of my colleagues and collaborators. Several years later, after living in LA for a couple of years and moving back to Vancouver, I connected with many of my old Seattle friends via Facebook. It was awesome catching up and seeing what they were up to.

Tara was a friend from Seattle. When I knew her, she was a talented up-and-coming screenwriter, who flew to LA frequently to pitch her ideas and take meetings. She seemed to be perennially close to selling her scripts but never quite managed to close a deal.

In the years since we had lost touch, I had left filmmaking behind, spent a few years doing digital production, and was now working at Vancity leading digital channels. When we reconnected on Facebook, I saw Tara was still in more or less the same position that she was in when we had lost touch. She was pitching her scripts, writing on spec (speculative writing, instead of getting paid beforehand on an assignment), flying to LA and taking meetings, but hadn't yet sold a screenplay or gotten anything produced.

I must admit, my heart broke a little. She's such an awesome, talented person, but seeing someone spend so many years aiming for success and not finding it seemed like delusion to me. After that long, if you're not successful, take a hint, move on and do something else. I, on the other hand, had listened to my feeling of delusion and left filmmaking behind, a career where I felt I was never going to be great. I had moved on with my life.

I loved filmmaking, was good at aspects of it, and had some talent, but knew deep down that I was not truly great at it. I met other filmmakers who were driven and talented in ways I was not (some were even willing to live in their cars). I went through a period of deep self-evaluation and honesty. So much of how I defined myself, and how others defined me, was as a filmmaker. After all of the self-work and making the difficult move out of filmmaking, being in touch with Tara, my former screenwriting colleague, made me uncomfortable. She struck a nerve.

Then something remarkable happened. One day, Tara posted on Facebook that she had sold a script. To a well-known director. Suddenly, she had real interest in her back log of scripts from her 15-plus years of writing. One of her spec scripts was named to an annual list of the top un-produced screenplays floating around LA. She was getting recognition, signing deals and moving forward, and I had never been so happy to be so wrong about anything. I was, and am, thrilled for her.

I also had to re-evaluate my own feelings. I had mistaken Tara's persistence for delusion. Her desire and commitment looked to me like failure and resistance to reality.

In creative endeavours, as in leadership, any adventure that is off the beaten path requires us to be persistent and fully believe in what we're doing. We have to strive for something in the face of adversity and others questioning our approach (and even our sanity). We can also go too far and become delusional. We can live in denial of the fact that what we're chasing will forever be elusive and unobtainable. This tension is completely fascinating to me.

No one can decide for us when persistence becomes delusion, or even if it ever does. It relies on our own conviction, our sense of purpose and ability for self-reflection, honesty, passion and curiosity. As long as we believe we must pursue something, and accept the risks and costs that such a pursuit entails, we have to keep going. Life is too short. At the same time, I also believe we have to check in on our progress with some frequency to ensure we are being realistic with ourselves—that we aren't staying on a course bound for nowhere.

It's tied to the sunk-cost fallacy where previously invested money, time or resources cause people to stick with something—a project that is going well over budget and won't yield intended results, for example—past the point where they should. Yet, abandoning something worthwhile because it's going through a rough patch isn't going to work out for us either.

Getting back in touch with Tara, I had imposed my own experiences onto her. I saw her persistence through my lens of leaving filmmaking behind when, in fact, she was still feeling the inspiration I used to feel when I stuck with something I believed in. Of course, I also didn't appreciate what she experienced during the years when we had lost touch—all the ups and downs, triumphs and heartaches that she went through in a fickle and sometimes cruel industry.

She still believed in her mission, and time proved her right. Tara's persistence could have been someone else's delusion. But it wasn't. Tara stuck with something she believed in and was 100% right in her commitment. I remain inspired by her resolve and self-awareness.

—

When I was leading digital channels at Vancity, I was visiting a branch one day when inspiration struck. In those days the tellers had televisions behind them playing the food network or the news network on mute with closed captioning. Those channels played all day long, every day. That day, when I was visiting a branch, there was a long line-up and one of the TVs was playing a commercial for a bank on the food network. That bothered me. Vancity is a credit union, and banks are its main competition. At a particularly busy time when members (what credit unions call their customers) were probably feeling a bit frustrated by the long wait, they were being offered an ad for a different financial institution.

Then, a few minutes later, the news network showed another ad for a different bank. I was certain that we could do something better with those TVs.

I started researching and building a business case for a private digital content distribution system via the TVs across all the branches. So, while people were in line they would see all the great things their business at Vancity was enabling in the community. I wanted to communicate the key differentiator and build pride in what the organization was doing.

The business case hit a brick wall. It required a fairly big investment, more than a million dollars; demonstrating a return on investment would be tricky and required a lot of assumptions. I knew it was not going to be an easy approval at the executive because it wasn't possible to show a direct correlation between displaying digital content in the branches with increases in people taking out mortgages or getting a new credit card. The business case required a bit more trust and faith.

Some people said I should drop it because it wasn't generating any interest. Instead I thought about how to create a sense of urgency about this work. I thought about how to lead to where I wanted to go, rather than just manage the creation of a business case and I began to socialize the proposal. I started getting coffee with executives and telling them about it, sharing my passion for the project, and not just focusing on the numbers and the potential cost and financial return. I found out that I had some advocates in the branch network who started asking about this idea when they saw senior leaders. I remained persistent because I believed in the idea and knew that all businesses would eventually have technology like this.

I could have given up, seen the chance of the business case being approved as delusional. Instead, because I really believed in the idea, I remained persistent. After presenting the idea and getting feedback a couple of times, I obtained full approval from the executive and the project rolled out to great success. It was a good example of not taking no for an answer when I knew an idea was right.

How do we know when we need to double down on an unpopular business case because we believe in it totally? Conversely, how do we know when we're pushing projects at our workplace that need to be thrown out? When do we need to rally others around an initiative that hasn't captured the imagination of the organization, but could still be needed? Part of seeing what level of influence you can achieve in an organization is to understand your record of being right about these things.

In so many ways, this is about developing self-awareness. If something doesn't go as planned stop and assess both the merits and downsides of the work you're doing, and also how you personally are behaving or being perceived (that last one is a doozy and yet is so critical). Having the emotional intelligence to understand all of those factors will elevate your ability to know when to stop, know what's really blocking your path and choose the best course of action as a result.

My desire was to be great at what I did. When I had the painful realization that I was never going to be a great filmmaker, I moved on to find things at which I could be great. If I had continued to believe in my filmmaking abilities and chances for success, I would have stuck it out longer.

In life, we have to balance the tenacity required to stick with something—not to give up on something too early just because it's difficult and hurts to pursue it—with the need to keep moving.

These experiences have taught me a lot about when to hold on and when to move on. I try to stay attuned to my own mindset—when is my pursuit of something persistence in face of adversity and when is it delusion, staying committed to something that is never going to happen?

—

Faulkner, Einstein and Newton.

There's a well-known (albeit untrue) story that the famed writer William Faulkner divorced his wife because she never understood that when he was at home just idly staring out the window, he was actually very hard at work. The work of creativity is celebrated as a light-bulb moment, as a hit of inspiration that we receive almost through divine intervention. This can happen, but in my experience it is extremely rare.

One time it did happen to me (as I described earlier in *Choosing The Music*) was after I had completed my long, gruelling and ultimately unsuccessful short film, *Greenwich Meridian*. I was living in Seattle and was on the bus on my way to my job at a motion picture laboratory — I was probably 25 at the time — when I had the idea for my short film *CheckMating*. The concept of the film came to me at once right down to the music I imagined playing behind the picture.

Most light-bulb moments come, like the Faulkner fable exemplifies, after periods of intense scrutiny, longing, contemplation and frustration. It often happens after meditating on an idea for prolonged periods of time, turning a concept over and over in your mind until something clicks. A lot of the time it feels like that moment when part of a song is swirling around inside your mind, you know you know the song, but you can't quite capture enough of the melody to place it. Or, when you are trying to think of the perfect word to express a thought you're having, but can't conjure it at that moment and only think of it once your mind is free to wander a bit. A lot of writing, a lot of many creative endeavours feel like that. In other words, a lot of it kind of sucks.

When it all comes together, when the idea emerges from the fog, when a scene clarifies itself, when a concept comes into sharp focus and you're entirely pleased with it, it is amazing. Many writers I know hate writing but love having written.

My own experience is that when I am doing creative work, I need to let the issues swirl around in my head and give myself a chance to just sit with the problem I'm facing and not try to actively solve it. Einstein once said, "If I had only one hour to save the world, I would spend fifty-five minutes defining the problem, and only five minutes finding the solution." In screenwriting, if I was trying to think of a way to get a character from one key scene to another, but couldn't figure out how to get them there in a way that felt authentic to the story, I just sat with that problem rolling it around, defining it.

—

We talk a lot about the *what* and the *how* of taking action, but not nearly enough about the *when*. If I'm focusing on a challenge at work, I use that same creative approach and will just let my mind wrestle with it. If I'm walking to work or taking a flight or going on a long drive, I ruminate on the issue. I don't really focus on solving it, I just roll it over and over in my mind. Soon enough, the issue works itself through, like undoing a knot, and the solution becomes clear (or at the very least, more clear).

The same is true for moments that challenge my leadership. If I am facing difficulty within the team, something that has to be handled delicately, I will allow myself space to daydream about the issue. Similar to Faulkner, I stare out the window looking perhaps like I'm doing nothing while my subconscious is working through the issue, mulling the pros and cons, and intended and unintended consequences, like a puzzle. I don't focus on the solutions, similar to the writer, who if they focus exclusively on solving a single script issue may get themselves bogged down in the myriad of details until they are immobilized; I focus merely on the challenge.

After some period of time doing that, and in my experience there's no way to rush it or to make it happen quickly, a moment of clarity emerges, and I will at least understand the issue better—which brings me one excellent step closer to a solution.

Isaac Newton *may* have dreamt up the theory of gravity after an apple hit him on the head, but if that apocryphal story is in any way true, he had likely been sitting under that apple tree for many parts of many days thinking about what holds everything pinned to the earth. The apple was representative of the moment of increased clarity, not the entire process of coming up with the theory.

It's about balancing natural talent with making an effort, allowing the two forces to work in tandem.

—

When I stopped making films, people would ask me if I missed it. I got that question for many, many years, and I reflected on it a lot. Deep down, although I missed elements of filmmaking—working with actors, being entrepreneurial, leading a truly creative pursuit—I didn't miss filmmaking. A lot of that had to do with my approach to starting a new project.

I would find myself writing a new script, almost unintentionally, putting plot points on post-it notes and fleshing out scenes and characters. Soon enough I would fill a wall of my home. Sometimes, the script ideas went nowhere, but some of them kept pestering me, picking at me to keep working on them. Those are the ones that became finished scripts.

If I was in the middle of one of those long slogs, waiting for sparks to fly, I used the light of those sparks however bright or dim, to light the next step of the path. Making a film is so complex; it can be hard to see too many steps in front of you, but being clear on the next two steps—and knowing that they will take you to a place where you can then see the two or three steps after that—is usually enough.

As a leader, I work hard to ensure that I move quickly to make progress. People are relying on me, I am accountable for moving many initiatives forward, and if I start to fall behind on something, work piles up like rush hour.

Sometimes, work comes up that I let slip. I procrastinate. Everyone does. I try not to, but it happens. What I have learned in my career is that when I miss a deadline, it is almost never an indication of laziness or a lack of productivity. I find delaying work is usually an intuitive and subconscious sense I have that the work needs more time. It needs to percolate and develop before I can take action. The *when* we do something can be as important as the *what* or the *how*. Maybe the work affects another team and they are too busy, or not ready, or not on the same page. Sometimes, things at an organization that I can't possibly know about change, opening the door for the work to proceed at a whole new pace or a completely different way than if I had marched ahead at the outset.

I have learned to listen closely to when I wait and when I procrastinate. In these moments my self-awareness is key to see if the challenge I'm facing is just tough, or icky, or problematic, and I just need to push through. Sometimes, however, something just doesn't feel right, like there's a puzzle piece still waiting to drop into place to give me a clearer picture of what needs to happen. That self-reflection has helped me find the right timing to move work forward and not spin my wheels and waste my team's time.

If I need to have a difficult conversation with a staff-member, the kind that can either help things improve or backfire and actually erode trust, I wait until the right moment to engage my colleague. I find a time when I feel clear about what I want to communicate and what I hope results from a challenging discussion. I also find a time when the other person seems ready to engage in that difficult conversation to maximize our chance of success. The *when* we have that conversation is so critical if the goal is to help people see their blind spots, understand performance issues and find ways to improve.

I have to be very self-aware about this, because that additional time could easily become complacency and reluctance to lean into work that just needs to get done, however challenging.

As I've said, I always made a film when I couldn't not make it. At some point I just didn't have that inspiration to create anymore. It wasn't that I stopped making films so much as I stopped feeling the pull and excitement of a new idea.

At the time I was leaving filmmaking behind, digital production and the web were taking off all around me in Seattle, and I was getting offers of work that I found challenging and interesting and that *gasp* paid well. It would have been negligent not to act on that unique moment I found myself in. My reflection and intuition paid off.

Part of acting on inspiration while working through a challenge is listening to signals around you to know which direction to go in at key forks in the road. There were film projects that, if I stopped pushing forward, all momentum would stop. If I stopped mentioning a project, no one would ask me about it. I had to make everything happen, and if the world pushed back too hard, I listened. That project just wasn't lighting up. Other times, projects caught fire and generated the energy I needed to help me move forward.

I see this as a kind of echolocation, where I send out signals to others about a new initiative or project and watch closely to see what cues come back to me. Positive signals will tell me a lot about the worthiness or readiness of the concept.

No reaction, let alone negative reactions will also tell me a lot about whether I'm pursuing something valuable.

When I transitioned from film to digital, I was at a point in my life when I didn't want to be the only person pushing things forward. I wanted to go with the flow; so, I lifted my feet, let the river take me with it and enjoyed that sense of momentum — of being part of a journey where I could work hard, add value and enjoy.

—

Let's revisit those two writer friends of mine, Peter and Terry. Terry put a note on his fridge, focused on his output and produced more than Peter, and also became better known. But there's another way to look at that story. Terry was very focused on external validation, on having his scripts developed and films sold. His commercial focus matured, but his artistry never did. Peter never gave in to those commercial forces and only produced when he heard the call of the Muses.

In hindsight, I'd rather be Peter than Terry. When I was writing *The Engagement Party*, I wanted to make a quirky, fun little film, something very personal. Through the rewriting process and visits to LA and discussions with agents and producers, I became more focused on making a film that could sell. I compromised some of the things I loved in earlier drafts of the script and started thinking about what the marketplace might receive. I sold out a little bit.

In the end, the film was neither that unique, personal film I wanted to make nor did it sell. I ended up with something compromised and that I didn't really love. I wish I had stayed true to my Peter side and given myself permission to pursue my own vision, rather than giving into my Terry side, which wanted success and validation.

I didn't know *The Engagement Party* would be my last film. It wasn't a conscious decision; it was a change in the tension between talent and effort. Instead of continuing to wait until the next spark struck, I took actions that led me down a different career path. I always felt that I would make another film when that passion came back, and it simply never did. The long slog had ended.

Well, almost. Here I am on a fall Sunday morning working on this book. Not because anyone is paying me to, or expecting me to, or pressuring me to. I am doing it because I can't not write this book. I am embracing a new kind of long slog, and it feels good.

—

Learn to pitch.

It's Jaws meets Titanic. The story of a boy and his horse surviving a flood-ravaged future. It's Romeo and Juliet during Nazi-occupied Warsaw.

"What's your elevator pitch?" That is a phrase I used to hear a lot. The origin of the term "elevator pitch" is uncertain, but many believe it started in the film industry. It is certainly highly associated with pitching a film concept.

There is no business like the film business when it comes to being able to take a script idea you have been working on — the narrative arc, character objectives, points of tension and conflict — and boil all of that down to a 45-second pitch. To succeed in film, you have to be able to sum up all that your project is and means in well under a minute. When you nail it, it's incredibly satisfying. People will want to read your script or take a meeting to discuss your project.

When I was making small, independent films in Seattle, I would take trips down to LA to meet with people in the film business. Before my first trip, I was nervous about going to the epi-centre of the industry. To get some perspective, I went for a walk with a fellow filmmaker who was several steps ahead of me in terms of selling his scripts and getting his career off the ground. He told me something that I will always remember.

He said that in Hollywood, everything is designed to make the person starting out feel like they have no power.

Everything reinforces the dominant power dynamic. You have meetings with agents in restaurants you can't afford—on the unspoken assumption they will foot the entire bill because if they didn't you wouldn't be able to afford to pay for your meal. What you drive and how new it is defines a big part of your status (if you drive an old Kia Rondo, park a few blocks away from the meeting so no one sees you parking—self-parking even, forget about valet!). Everything plays out to make you feel like you have no power or control and that the person you're meeting with has it all.

My filmmaking mentor told me that all of that display of authority rests upon one simple reality: The wealth and power of those in charge would come to a sharp halt if they didn't have creative talent like actors, directors and writers creating new content to drive their cycles of revenues and prosperity. The executives don't create anything, they enable everything that is created.

When I went to LA, I had to see myself as a potential creative talent that those in power required to be in constant supply. I had to believe I possessed something they needed.

With that advice, I shifted my entire perception of the power dynamic. I took meetings with the confidence that I had at least as much of what they needed, new creative content and talent, as they had what I wanted. It didn't always feel true, but I focused on reframing that dynamic and kept it top of mind. This new perspective helped give me confidence when I had meetings with important players.

As a result of my attitude, I got a lot of meetings and felt a real sense of progress.

Having said that, we also need to ensure that we are pitching the right information at the right level. When I was making all those trips from Seattle to LA, having meetings felt like progress. I had a contact at Miramax—the absolute king and king-maker in the indie-film world at the time—who would meet with me on my visits. She would read my scripts and watch my films. I always imagined that I was cultivating an important relationship, and it certainly stroked my ego that I could get meetings at Miramax. That made me feel very important.

Looking back, I realize now that my contact at Miramax was incredibly nice and patient, but too junior to either move my work forward or cut me loose. What felt like progress was just a series of steady-state meetings and discussions; nothing would have transpired with her. Had she seen something of greater promise in my work, she only had the authority to pass me along to someone above her in the hierarchy. Likewise, she couldn't alienate me in case I turned out to be the next Tarantino. Her job was to keep contacts like me warm, neither promising too much nor letting me cross the street to talk with a different company.

When I started working in the corporate world, I reflected on that power dynamic. Instead of getting nervous in front of owners, executives or board members, I assumed I was someone they needed: smart, committed talent who could be the future leadership of the organization (I didn't let this become arrogance, because no one likes arrogance).

Work is simply an exchange of value. They have value, and so do I. I refuse to accept a power imbalance in my own perception, as that can lead to feelings of victimization, or a lack of agency over my work and career. If the executive feels the need to puff up that power imbalance, I note it, because that says a lot about whether they are someone I want to work with or not.

When I meet with my staff now, as CEO, I take the other side of that equation. The team needs a leader, for sure, but without the team how long would things continue to function? The organization can survive longer without me than without them, that's for sure. As a leader who thinks about succession planning, finding staff with ambition and skill is essential. We only discover that if we spend time with each other and meet as equals, and remove as much of the power dynamic as possible.

As a leader, I invest a lot of time in my people. I also keep my Miramax experience top of mind. I don't want anyone reading anything unintentional into my time with them. Time with me doesn't mean you're going to automatically get that next assignment or promotion. It doesn't mean you have special access; all my team has equal access. I also meet staffers for whom I'm the first executive they have ever sat down with one-on-one. I don't want to intimidate them. I want them to feel like we're all colleagues who have different roles to play in achieving our collective goals.

So, life involves pitching to executives. Although I kind of hated it, I learned to always have two or three pitches ready just in case I needed to pull one out. It's critical to have something of value to offer when you're pitching — to have confidence that no matter how junior you are, you have something that the company needs: up and coming talent.

Today, I like it when staff has a short narrative of a key initiative they're working on in case they find themselves in the elevator with me and I happen to ask them, "What are you working on these days?"

—

Today's intern is tomorrow's executive.

One of my favourite experiences that demonstrates the true importance of being a decent human being to other people—not because of role, title or position—concerns an intern I worked with at a dot.com in Seattle in 2000.

My career in film had segued nicely into roles in digital and web production. One of the companies I worked for on my way out of being a filmmaker was an online film distributor based in Seattle. It was a great company, and they had actually successfully distributed my own short film *CheckMating*—getting it seen all over the world.

All good things come to an end. In March 2000, when the dot.com bubble burst, jobs in Seattle went from plentiful to scarce pretty much overnight. The company I worked for was bought by a competitor in San Francisco, and although a few people re-located, the rest of us were given notice. That was the impetus I needed to move to LA, where my wife attended a teaching program and I took the gamble that my background in film and experience doing digital projects would make me marketable.

In those days at the dot.com, when many people were boxing up their belongings, stealing the office furniture, and leaving the company, one of my colleagues brought in an intern to help him with his work. It was a weird move, but somehow he got approval, and the intern allowed him to do absolutely nothing all day while he collected his last few paycheques. He handed all his remaining work to the intern.

The intern, Ajay, was super bright and ambitious, and he was trying to decide whether to go back to school for journalism or stay in the corporate world. He made the most of his time with us and did truly excellent work. Ajay made a lasting impression on me. One day we were having lunch at a burger place on Seattle's waterfront when I choked on a french fry, and he performed a successful Heimlich maneuver on me and possibly saved my life.

When the company finally shuttered its Seattle office and moved the few remaining people and assets to San Francisco, I remember there was literally one good job opening in town. It was at Microsoft as a digital producer. I must have known 20 people who were applying for it, and I was very glad to be moving to LA and not competing.

In the end, Ajay, the intern at the dot.com won the job. I was very happy for him, and I remember thinking that it was interesting that Microsoft, in the face of some pretty extensive and impressive resumes, went for the young, inexperienced—and therefore inexpensive—resource. He was lucky to get the job, and I was thrilled for him.

I lost touch with Ajay for a few years, but he ended up doing very well for himself. He moved up at Microsoft and worked there for several years before ending up at a large television network, where he oversaw digital production.

That television network had hired Ajay as part of a move to increase their digital content. They ramped up production, brought in new talent and started acquiring companies for their content libraries. One of their acquisitions was the dot.com where Ajay and I had worked—where Ajay had once been an intern.

I found this to be amazing—he left the company as an intern and a few short years later, Ajay negotiated the acquisition of that company and ended up overseeing it as part of the division he ran at a large television network. I hope all those remaining staffers who were still at the dot.com had been nice to Ajay, because no one could have imagined that the bright young intern would be their CEO's boss in just five years.

—

When you're in a specific industry, even a city as large as LA can, at times, feel like a small town. When I worked for a digital marketing agency in LA, the firm had a very lucrative contract with Sony Pictures, and the biggest project in the shop at the time was for the website and digital promotion of *Bad Boys 2*. The website launch date was looming and the client wanted to make a lot of changes before it went live, which put a lot of extra pressure on the staff. The project manager was at lunch on a patio in Pacific Palisades complaining about the project, about Sony, even about Michael Bay, the film's director. He was blowing off steam. It turns out, Michael Bay's mom was sitting at a nearby table, heard the complaining and told her son. It created a huge crisis at the firm and almost lost them their contract with Sony. Although I wasn't present for that lunch and wasn't working on the *Bad Boys 2* website, it taught me to be discreet. Even in a city as massive as LA, you never know who (or whose mom) might be at a table within earshot when you think you're just venting to a colleague.

I'm nice to people, and not just because I may work for them one day. But it sure helps. The golden rule absolutely applies. That kid who is a smart intern on your team, who you ignore and maybe even treat poorly, may one day be your boss. Or your boss' boss.

When I was at Vancity, I worked with a VP who was so sure that when his boss retired he would be promoted into that position that he didn't focus as much as he should have on how he treated his colleagues and fellow VPs. He acted superior to his peers because he seemed certain of his path. When his boss did retire the CEO made a shuffle at the executive level and one of the other VPs, whom he had treated disrespectfully, was now his boss. Needless to say his new boss didn't wait too long before she disciplined the behaviour she saw in him as a direct peer. You never know when a move like that can happen, so best not to assume you know your path too well.

—

When I first moved to LA, there was an article going around that helped me understand the culture of the city. The article described powerful agents and producers who treated people rudely, humiliating them, making them feel small at every opportunity. The result of that wasn't a backlash towards treating others with decency, oh no, quite the opposite. This terrible behaviour from those in power led people with no power to start treating others poorly, merely to look important. Treating people rudely became a power move. As a result, people who had absolutely no power or authority over anything would stop returning your calls or stand you up for coffee, just because they mistakenly thought it made them look powerful—at least more powerful and in demand than you were. It was a truly revolting trend.

It became a "thing" to emulate the petty, mean ways that important people could act in a city hell-bent on accumulating and displaying power. I never found this behaviour attractive. I think there's more power in treating people well, dealing with them fairly and building relationships based on mutual respect and reciprocity. Having power or access to power may mean that you can stand someone up for coffee or not return their calls and get away with it for a period of time, but it isn't a way to conduct yourself.

In the end, all we know is that we're human beings trying to eke out some happiness in our lives. The most important thing is to be decent and kind to other people—not because of your role, title or position—but because we're all equal. If it helps, think of the intern who may become your peer or even your boss one day, and ask yourself if you treated them with respect on their way up.

—

Toss the script.

Most directors rely very little on improvisation, and instead stick to the script methodically. Some however, see the script only as a leaping-off point and work with the actors to improvise scenes and dialogue in line with the script's motivations.

It was said that Alfred Hitchcock found filmmaking to be a tedious affair. He was known to meticulously plan every scene, storyboarding everything ahead of time and working out each beat thoroughly. The actual filmmaking was simply going through the motions to capture everything he had already completely pre-planned.

Another great British filmmaker, Mike Leigh, spends a ton of time with his actors before shooting begins and throughout the filmmaking process to improvise much of the script and scenes to form the final film.

That may sound like an either/or situation; as a filmmaker you either improvise or you don't, but filmmaking is a lot more nuanced that that. On any given film, there are times when improvisation works and times when it's best to stick to the script. Even those filmmakers who adopt an improvisational style, and allow for a lot of looseness and freedom among the actors on set, invariably use some kind of script as a foundation.

Very few directors completely improvise a film with no sense of what they're going to shoot. Conversely, no successful director plans everything so completely that they leave no room for creative inspiration and spontaneity on set — I bet even Alfred Hitchcock did this at least a little bit.

The script is used as a set of blueprints to understand where the narrative is going. It is a plan to determine where a key scene fits into the overall story-arc and how all of the elements will come together. A script, and the work done to interpret that script, is key to understanding characters' motivations and relationships. All of that prep is instrumental to helping a film transcend the original words on paper and to holding an audience's interest. As discussed in the chapter *Understand The Subtext*, it is the interpretation of a script that allows a film to speak to the part of our souls that require stories to better understand the world around us and to make sense of the people and events in our lives.

The script is foundational. Without it, actors wouldn't understand their characters, investors wouldn't know what they were investing in, a cinematographer wouldn't be able to best frame and light a shot and an editor would be lost in how to assemble the footage.

It is imperative that everyone understands the script; it is the director's job to help them understand it in the same way. But for an actor, once the script is memorized, interpreted and internalized, it can sometimes be thrown away.

What do I mean by throw the script away? An actor's job is to deeply understand and incorporate their character's motivation within any given scene. Once they know that, if different words come out of their mouth, it can often improve the scene. In that moment, knowing all that they do about the character and what they want, if the actor says something off-script, it usually comes from a place of real truth (searching for the truth, after all, is the artist's main job).

That moment of improvisation can be glorious and can elevate a scene tremendously. That kind of improvisation, however, only comes from chewing through the script over and over, memorizing every word, knowing every intention and extracting every bit of meaning and subtext. Only with all that exploration and deep character work behind them can an actor's improvisation really extend the meaning of the words and get to a scene's deeper truth. In that moment, the script can be tossed aside.

When I think of improvisation, I often think of equivalents in other media. Some of the great abstract, impressionist and surrealist painters had deep schooling in the "rules" of painting. They could paint in a way that demonstrated their mastery of technique. They knew the schools of thought that had proceeded them. For many of them, if you look at their early work, it is more rigid, structured and accurate. Early works by Picasso, Dali and Pollock show that they learned the "correct" way to paint.

If you trace their evolution as artists, their own inspired techniques and styles slowly affect their paintings, bending them away from traditional methods and more to their own original styles. You can see the emergence of something unique, something that would become embodied by their names, something *Daliesque* or *Picassoesque*. They had to learn the rules to break them.

If the idea is to do something so truly unique that you don't have to learn what came before, then you have to be more brilliant than anyone else—by orders of magnitude. It is possible, but incredibly rare, and you would have to be a bigger genius than Picasso.

In the editing room, a specific cut can take a long time. Choosing the exact moment to leave one shot and cut to the next for maximum impact can require many, many attempts to perfect. Sometimes it takes a while because an actor's eye-line, where they are looking, goes off slightly, and you want to cut away before they do that. Other times, they have an expression that speaks volumes and you want to to cut to that look exactly as a specific word comes out of another actor's mouth offscreen. The goal is to maximize what's great within the footage and minimize distractions or moments that don't work as well.

It can be painstaking. Over time, I developed a strong discipline with my editing technique and could pick a point, almost at random, to cut to the next shot and it would be perfect. By honing my skills and talent, I developed a stronger feeling for the footage and the scene, and I learned to trust my instincts to guide me to something brilliant very quickly.

In all of these examples, you have to know exactly *what* you're doing and *why* you're doing it. Only then, can you throw the *how* to the wind and take some interesting chances to improvise something inspired.

—

In business, I have known people who were promoted very quickly and relatively young. They skipped a lot of the steps of basic management, and didn't pay their dues leading small teams, and then larger and larger groups doing work of increasing complexity, output and value. That slow and steady progression builds muscles, earns you battle scars and teaches you lessons. As leaders, we need to experience those times when our choices worked out wonderfully, as well as those times when we made mistakes and created more problems than we solved.

As I mentioned in the chapter *Be An Imposter*, before my first role at the executive level, the largest team I had ever led was 30 people. When I was promoted to the executive level, I oversaw 1,800 people in over 60 locations across the entire region where we did business. It required me to use the skills I had gained in previous roles, but scale them up significantly. I needed to quickly adopt a very different leadership style.

I had always relied on my communication skills and interpersonal strengths to build confidence in what we were doing. I did this partly by naming the elephants in the room that were distracting people but no one was openly talking about. I focused on connecting with people to understand them and how to best motivate them. These traits and behaviours had always served me well. Now, I would meet only a fraction of the people I led. I had to learn to lead people through layers and layers of other people.

I used the skills I had gained through years of managing and leading and adapted them, improvising based on knowing that previous script. I started conducting conference calls with the VPs who reported to me and the entire division of 1,800 employees. I wanted opportunities for the leadership team to communicate with everyone all at once and open the conversation to questions and comments. No one had done that in the organization before. I took the way I communicated in small teams and found ways to adjust my style, which had previously brought me success —to a massive new role.

My own leadership skills had to be developed and expanded, and I found myself in situations that I could only work through because of all the lessons and techniques I had learned through prior experience and training.

When I see leaders who were promoted young, I usually see a leader with lumps. In some areas, they are very gifted and strong; that's the reason they were promoted so quickly. I also see areas in which they are under-developed and weak, areas where they have yet to be tested and don't have enough lived experience. Some work through that, stay humble, are self-aware and build out those areas and reduce their lumpiness over time. Others develop an armour of arrogance, building only on their already impressive strengths while ignoring their weaknesses. In these cases, their lumps become more pronounced and problematic. They develop asymmetrically in a way that will ultimately hold them back.

As leaders, we need to work through the levels, take lateral moves to gain new skills or lead in different areas. We have to think like painters who learn classical techniques for years before they break out their own style. Our careers are marathons, not a sprint.

We need to remain focused on building out our full leadership potential to avoid those lumps and be as free of blind spots as we possibly can. We have to learn our scripts deeply, interpreting them, understanding them fully so we can throw them away and gain the benefits of improvising based on whatever comes our way.

—

Understanding Shakespeare.

Something that used to make my brain hurt was shooting a scene, a specific shot that has to work as its own moment, and balancing that moment with knowing how that scene fits into the entire arc of the film. When you work with an actor on something very specific, like a single line of dialogue or how they enter a scene, you must remain cognizant not only of the moment being filmed, but also of the previous time the audience saw that character, what they had been doing since then off camera, and what is coming up next for them. If the actor has a big revelation later in the film, what can you do in this scene to foreshadow that? Or, do the opposite; do something that heightens the tension when that moment is revealed.

You have to be aware of the minute detail as well as the whole. You have to make this the best square of fabric you can, while never losing sight of the entire quilt.

That's the role of leadership: Balancing what needs to be done in the moment with the overarching goals and strategies you are pursuing.

It's easy to get wrapped up in a great project or initiative and lose sight of the fact that people are overworked and that this project, however good, may be one of several your team is juggling at any given moment. My job as a leader is to determine which are the best initiatives to help us make progress toward our goals as an organization.

Time is finite. Resources are finite.

—

When I joined the Community Investment team at Vancity, where we invested money into community projects and organizations that do good work aligned with the organization's pillars of change, I naively thought that we would give money to good causes and opportunities and say no to ones that were less good. Was I ever wrong.

I quickly learned that almost everything we looked at was important, well thought through, and necessary. We said "yes" to highly aligned projects that were ready for the money now; we said "no" or "not yet" to organizations that were slightly less aligned with our objectives or needed more time to develop.

Sometimes we would answer a request for $60,000 with $8,000 for the organization to hire a consultant to flesh out the idea more and develop a stronger plan so they would be in a better place to receive the $60,000 they were looking for down the line. Or we would offer funds to help them figure out how to diversify their income stream and set up a social enterprise so they wouldn't need that $60,000 as a handout again.

We had to give a grant application enough attention and care that we could understand the project and could evaluate it and possibly get behind it, while simultaneously holding that potential investment against the frame of our overall community strategy. We had to look at this individual piece of fabric against the whole quilt.

—

Have you ever seen a production of Shakespeare and, even though the language was foreign and unfamiliar, you understood every line? If you've seen great Shakespeare, you probably have. On the other hand, have there been times when you were attending a performance in modern English and felt completely lost and had no idea what was going on?

The difference between the two is that the director, actors, lighting technicians, and sound designers in the Shakespeare production above were all clear about what the play meant to them and could translate that meaning into every single moment—every lighting cue, sound effect and costume choice.

That deep understanding drove clarity, and that clarity drove decisions that best exemplified the meaning of the play. That drive took energy, experience, patience and persistence to ensure that every choice was the best possible one to move things forward. When that happens the audience can experience that effort, and they get it; they follow everything.

Conversely, when that doesn't happen—if the cast, crew or director wasn't talented enough or they didn't work hard enough or they weren't seasoned enough to understand the play entirely and translate that understanding into consistent clarity—the audience can tell. The modern production may have had some individual moments that broke through and were incredible, but the whole play probably didn't hold up.

Some things link the big picture with those small details. When I was getting ready to shoot *The Engagement Party*, a film colleague advised me to have great hot food on set for lunch. They explained that if people sit down for lunch and the food is cold and not very good, the cast and crew will start to complain about the food. Once the complaining starts, people will continue complaining about all sorts of things. People will complain about the script, the director, the pay or talk about the other film shoots they could be on instead. When complaining like that takes root, morale will suffer. In a workplace, it's toxic. Give people a good, hot meal and it will prevent all kinds of other complaints. It was great advice and as a result we focused on providing terrific meals on set every day.

Now that I'm running an organization, I invest a lot of energy into elements that improve well-being like paid time off, benefits packages, flexible schedules and ensuring the Staff Engagement Committee is well-resourced. Ensuring those softer parts of the workplace are high functioning keeps the culture strong and the employees happy. These things prevent staff from feeling those small, sometimes inevitable things that go wrong in a complex environment and reduce doubt about the big picture stuff.

Similar to what was covered in the *Understand The Subtext* chapter, if a director doesn't understand the script they're shooting, or the film they're making, then how will they make a film that is comprehensible? If you, as a leader don't understand your organization's strategies, mission and current three-year plan, how can you lead a team to execute with excellence? You have to know that big picture and link it to the myriad decisions, both big and small, to make sure your team performs its role with brilliance. Keeping an eye on the details while ensuring alignment with the big picture is one of the most challenging balancing acts of leadership. It's enough to make your brain hurt, but it's one of our key responsibilities as leaders.

—

Kill your babies.

Being on a film set involves a lot of hurry-up-and-wait. A lot of standing around, making small talk, trying to keep energy up, and snacking while lighting rigs get set up, cameras get focused, set decorations get put in exactly the right spot, and checks get made against previous shots to make sure continuity is good (to ensure that an actor's sleeves weren't buttoned up in the last shot but are now unbuttoned).

After all that waiting and prepping, the scene is finally ready, and people dive into action to shoot the take. It's an environment where people are starved for entertainment because of all the time spent waiting around.

Sometimes, an actor, often an actor who through all that waiting around entertains the troops and becomes really well liked by the cast and crew, delivers a key line in a perfect way that has everyone on set rolling with laughter. The moment is so funny that there can be a risk of the crew's laughter being picked up by the boom mic. The mood on set tells you that the actor totally nailed it and everyone knows you have that perfect take.

Weeks later in the editing room, the director remembers that moment when the actor nailed it. They assemble that take in the midst of the rest of the shots in the scene, and let it play. And guess what... it doesn't work. It was hysterical on set but it doesn't fit into the actual scene. It was a case of *you had to be there*. It was a moment of immense joy and release on set, but it doesn't translate through the lens to an audience.

Filmmaking, at the end of the day, is comprised of a constant stream of choices the director must make. What separates an amateur filmmaker from a seasoned filmmaker, in many ways, comes down to their ability to make decisions based on their own good taste.

If an artist, whether a writer, filmmaker, painter or poet, has good taste and applies their taste consistently, then they will be making choices on what to include, what to play around with, what interesting avenues to follow—and also what to cut out. It was said that Michelangelo looked at a huge block of marble and could see the sculpture held within it. He *merely* cut out all the stone that wasn't the sculpture—held invisible to the rest of us within that huge piece of rock. He made choices about what to remove and what to leave in place—what was mere rock and what was his sculpture hiding within, waiting to be revealed.

This is a key lesson I had to learn, and unfortunately frequently relearn, in my days of filmmaking. I would leave in scenes, shots, takes or moments that we worked so hard to capture and which played so well to cast and crew on set but—if I was more honest with myself—did not play well in the finished film.

My first screening of the film would usually be for the cast and crew, and those moments got the yells, shouts and peels of laughter, evoking such joyous memories of the set. That screening always felt so good. The moments that elicited such a great reaction in the cast and crew screening, however, were those same moments that often fell dead in front of strangers.

An audience doesn't care about how much fun people had on set when that actor turned and raised his eyebrow, and delivered a line that everyone loved. I should have had the experience and maturity to know the difference and save it for a cast and crew outtake reel and leave it out of the finished narrative.

That lesson was very hard for me. I wanted to leave in all the bits I was proud of, instead of only those that best served the story. There were times when we worked so hard to get a shot just right, but the scene should have been cut to keep the film's pacing tight and moving forward. Keeping the shot might show how brilliant the cinematographer and I were, but it distracted from the film and ultimately pulled the audience out of the narrative. I wanted them to get lost in the film, not think about how well it was made.

Great writers like Hemingway would call this *killing your babies*. Those scenes, turns of phrase or pieces of dialogue that the creator loved and was so proud of but had to be excised to keep the reader or the audience hooked.

—

In business, we get attached to pet projects. We invest time into initiatives that aren't part of the organization's strategy or that don't make it through the next stage-gate. I've worked with people who kept their project hidden because they knew they weren't approved. Every company I've worked for has struggled to shut down projects that aren't working. People often want less work on their plates, unless it's the work *they* care about.

At Brightside, in order to be able to offer someone affordable housing at a rate where they pay 30% of their income on rent, we have to evaluate a resident's income annually to make sure they qualify. When I started at the organization, what I observed was that our process for evaluating resident income was broken. It wasn't a good experience for the residents or for staff. It was cumbersome and intrusive. The income review coordinator who was accountable for this function seemed frustrated and unhappy in their role. We would ask them about small ways to tweak the role but were often met with a lack of interest in change and sometimes resistance.

As a management team, we decided to put an end to the process, which would eliminate the income review coordinator role. The head of HR and I met with them to have a mature discussion about the changes that we were about to bring in. We told them that these changes would eliminate their role, but that we had a different role we would like them to take on. I wasn't sure how they would react; in the past they hadn't always been open to small changes and now we were proposing a much bigger change.

They were quiet during the discussion, asked a few questions and the meeting ended without incident. To their great credit, once the news settled in and they knew the changes were going to be big, they started working with us to overhaul the income review process and migrate to their new role. Their recommendations were smart and actionable. Killing the existing, long-standing process opened the door to the innovation we needed, and renewed the employee's engagement in a new role.

Renewal is part of business and part of life.

This is the experience a filmmaker learns when they cut out fun moments that don't serve the overall film. A leader needs to be willing to reexamine why and how they do things and be prepared to stop doing things that no longer serve the organization's mission and strategy.

The term *Kill Your Babies* is a very tough one to write because it's such a horrible phrase. When a tough decision is in front of me to cut out a scene that I love and am proud of—and may have cost a lot of time and money to create—for the sake of the whole film I think of it as a small death. I don't take it lightly. I also don't avoid it when it's necessary. We shouldn't do it easily, but sometimes we have to.

—

Tell your story.

The key job of any artist is to tell a story steeped in deep truths. That story may take the form of a painting that makes you feel something and shakes up a belief you have, or a symphony that transports you out of your world only to be able to see it—even momentarily—from a different perspective.

Leaders should attempt these same things. We need to speak clearly and honestly about what we're striving for. We should inspire. Our 50,000 years of human behaviour tells us over and over again that nothing inspires more than stories.

As a leader, your job is to tell stories, and inspire change and development for you, your staff, your board, your customers, your partners and, ultimately, your organization as a whole. The stories you tell should be full of meaning and connection.

Is your career telling a story? Is the story of your work or industry a story you are proud of and believe in? If so, you're in a good place and on a good path. If it isn't, then look at how you can make a change.

When someone comes to me for career advice and I hear their current work woes, I sometimes see them as stuck in the wrong story. It isn't necessarily a bad story, but it is evident that it is the wrong story for them. If we don't see or care enough to recognize that we're living the wrong story, we need to work to change that. I have become allergic to such situations. I have quit perfectly good jobs with no back up plan because I just didn't believe in the story of that company and couldn't ethically live it or honestly tell it.

—

Why did I ultimately leave filmmaking behind? I found that an awful lot of filmmaking culture was based on seeking success first in order to obtain happiness later. I have shared multiple examples of attempting to find fulfillment through external success; with that success and validation being defined and adjudicated by other people, mostly people with whom I shared few values. The goalposts of that success kept moving so that even if I had found it, the feeling would be fleeting because I felt compelled to seek out more and greater success before I could find any real happiness. In that way, I would never be happy.

If I made a film, my feeling of fulfillment would be short-lived because the industry culture would push me to want to make a bigger and more successful film. The idea of being an independent filmmaker who keeps making small, personal films one after another was illusory and incredibly difficult to maintain (equivalent to the neighbourhood musician who plays local gigs and has a small regional following). I needed to escape that pursuit and define my own values to live by, to reverse the equation. I didn't need success to be happy, I needed to understand what made me happy and through seeking fulfillment, create success that was personal and real. I couldn't do that in the dominant culture of The Business. Maybe others could, but I couldn't.

The curiosity and passion that has guided me throughout my life has found a home at Brightside. I find it exceedingly worthwhile and meaningful to use my talents and energy to provide homes for people who might otherwise fall into homelessness. I find tremendous fulfillment living my values, in a city I love each and every day. It provides me the meaning I found making films, and enables me to live out the mission that Amy and I discovered on Venice Beach. It lets me define success for myself and live a happy life as a result.

For the last 15 years of my career, I have sought to work for people and organizations whose stories fit perfectly with my own story. I have learned to seek out organizations whose stories are not just compelling, but morally just, and important. That is my goal in life and at work. I hope that my story is one that reflects my values as a person—who I am as a leader, an employee, a colleague, a neighbour, a family member and a friend.

For some, mixing the personal and the professional is uncomfortable. For me it is inevitable, so we had best learn to grapple with it. If you are struggling with this, try thinking about work-life balance in a different way. I try not to think in terms of work-life balance, I think instead about work-life integration. I am one integrated person who spends a lot of my time at work with colleagues and a lot of my time at home with family. I want those two sides of me to be not just in balance, but have a sense of wholeness.

I do that by taking the things I love to do and embed the lessons and values of those things into my work as a leader. It makes me more human, more empathetic, and also gives me advantages. It makes me creative and agile. It makes people want to work with me.

My journey as a filmmaker was critical to understanding the way we live our stories. The greatest gift I received from being a filmmaker was learning this lesson. Even though I don't make films anymore, I carry this knowledge as part of my story in my life and through my career as a "Buisnessman".

In the end, perhaps the clearest lesson is the one we started with: Do what you love (and the money *may* follow). If you can figure out what you love, focus on that and try and bring it into your career.

Do you love cooking? Or knitting? Or playing hockey? Spend some time meditating on what about that activity makes you want to do it and to set aside your valuable time to pursue it. I can't emphasize that enough. My entire career has been built on applying lessons from filmmaking to the worlds of digital media, cooperative banking, and community housing. My guess is that if you explore an area where you have passion and are curious about why you love to do that thing, you will be able to translate that into your work and integrate your world in a way that is powerful and fulfilling.

For me, it has been a way to explore the intersection of passion and profession. It's a noble ambition to bring that authenticity to work as a leader, to bring creativity and curiosity to the way we manage, coach, and lead. My background is a rare one in a corporate setting, and I hope I have brought out some examples that reveal some truths about who we are at work and in life, and how we can help each other develop.

I have long believed that it is critically important to find alternative styles of leadership and get away from the bland and ordinary ways that leadership is taught, (mis)understood, and applied. Instead we should seek to focus on self-awareness and reflection, and emphasize our passion, curiosity, and creativity in the workplace. We are just humans bumbling around, trying to find meaning, and to do our best. The sooner our workplaces can embrace that reality and expect people to be curious, interesting, unusual, individual, vulnerable, sometimes fragile, and exceptional, the sooner we will have flourishing workplaces that are innovative, welcoming, and creative.

That's why I wrote this book. I crave to see workplaces where there is greater diversity in thought and approach among leaders; where we embrace creativity to unlock innovation; where we are passionate about our organization's values and the stories connected to those values that inspire action. Having a creative perspective, rather than everyone utilizing the traditional way of working and leading, serves us all better.

I appreciate anyone who read this book. I hope there are some parallels that proved useful, interesting, illustrative, and entertaining. I hope it may inspire more leaders to ponder if their leadership reflects who they are, their own journeys, passions, and values. I hope it inspires people to make some changes that will create happier, healthier and more productive and creative workplaces.

Thank you.

—

Closing credits.

When I was 17 and starting to make short videos for the amusement of my friends—to try and finagle class credit—I had already fallen in love with the young woman whom I would later marry. Although we had already known each other for a few years in high school, Amy and I started dating after graduation and our relationship deepened through my early struggling years of independent filmmaking. When I started gravitating towards the relatively new field of web and digital production, I had already been married to Amy for a few years. I write this now having pivoted careers a few times and landing in a place that is both unexpected and amazing. Amy and I are still happy and married. I am grateful to have someone to live my life with who is true to our shared inner spirit and the things that guide us as people, rather than the trappings of career. I love you Amy, you are extraordinary.

My lifelong friend Asaf inspired me to make films in the first place. His friendship, honesty, creativity, humour, and ambition have always been critical to me as a guide and as a person. None of the stories in this book would have happened if we hadn't become close friends in high school. I wouldn't be the person I am without his friendship and influence today.

Without Tim M., and Matt D., and my beloved former Credit Union Water Cooler crowd, I wouldn't have had a platform to give the initial presentation that this book was based on. Our community nurtured me, was essential to me, and I appreciate you all. This is for you.

I want to thank all of the real people behind the stories: Tara, Ajay, Rob, Peter, Terry, Mr. Barabond, Lilly, and the waiter from the West Hollywood hot spot (some of them know who they are, others likely don't). They each taught me important lessons, albeit sometimes by accident.

I am deeply grateful to all the colleagues, bosses, and direct reports I've had at so many different organizations and businesses over the years. Thanks to Linda M. and Tamara V. for being such great bosses and mentors to me, and to Christine B. for being all three: a great co-worker, employee, and boss! I already feel guilty leaving so many others unnamed.

Alison L. is the best executive coach I could have found and am grateful for her continual help, support, and perspective.

Thanks to Alison A. who read so many drafts of this book all along the way and whose editing expertise helped me to shift it from a bunch of stories into a book. To Michael S., John H., Sam R., Susan B., Liam G., Sarah C.-K., and Raevn B. who read various drafts and helped me to see the forest for the trees, and whose insights helped me take my idea further than I had imagined.

I'm grateful to my friend Andrew H. for designing the book cover.

I want to thank my mother Sima and my sister Devorah, who both demonstrated to me that we should each follow our own paths and do what we love to do. I am grateful that my father Paul introduced me to film and filmmaking in a meaningful, long-lasting way.

Finally, I want to express my deep gratitude and love to my son Ivan. His ethical core, devotion to his music and his relentless individuality have taught me so much about myself. He inspires me to be true to myself every day.

—

About the author.

William Azaroff is the CEO of Brightside Community Homes Foundation, an organization dedicated to making housing accessible for those who struggle to meet the demands of market housing in Vancouver, one of the most unaffordable cities on the planet.

He was a long-time executive at Vancity, performing multiple leadership roles at the community-focused credit union serving the financial needs of their half million member-owners and the communities where they live and work.

William sits on the board of the BC Non-Profit Housing Association, the provincial umbrella organization for the non-profit housing sector and was board chair of Modo, a car-sharing co-operative, and the Vancity Community Foundation.

This is his first book.

www.azaroff.com   @wazaroff

www.ingramcontent.com/pod-product-compliance
Lightning Source LLC
Chambersburg PA
CBHW071500220526
45472CB00003B/872